Corpses,
Coffins,
and Crypts

Corpses, Coffins, and Crypts

· A History of Burial ·

Penny Colman

Henry Holt and Company New York

Henry Holt and Company, LLC
Publishers since 1866
115 West 18th Street
New York, New York 10011

Published in Canada by Fitzhenry & Whiteside Ltd.,
195 Allstate Parkway, Markham, Ontario L3R 4T8.

Library of Congress Cataloging-in-Publication Data
Colman, Penny.
Corpses, coffins, and crypts : a history of burial / by Penny Colman.
p.   cm.
Includes bibliographical references and index.
Summary: Documents the burial process throughout the centuries and
in different cultures.
1. Funeral rites and ceremonies—History—Juvenile literature.
2. Burial—Juvenile literature.   3. Death—Social aspects—Juvenile
literature.   [1. Funeral rites and ceremonies—History.   2. Burial
customs—History.]   I. Title.
GT3150.C58   1997   393'.09—dc21   97-7842

ISBN 0-8050-5066-3
First Edition—1997
Designed by Meredith Baldwin

Printed in the United States of America
on acid-free paper.∞
10 9 8 7 6 5

Excerpts from Dr. Kenneth V. Iserson's *Death to Dust: What Happens to Dead Bodies?*, Galen
Press, Ltd., 1994, reprinted with permission of Galen Press, Ltd., Tucson, AZ.

Acknowledgments

Regardless of how preoccupied and intense I got as I researched, wrote, and took photographs for this book, my indispensable friend Linda Hickson kept me anchored with her zest for life and willingness to trek through cemeteries; talk about corpses, coffins, and crypts; and read every draft of the manuscript. At different times during the process, other friends and family members pitched in, too, including Stephen Colman, David Colman, Jonathan Colman, Katrin de Haën, Dana Bilsky, Jeremy Bilsky, John Granberry, Elizabeth Skurnick, Gay Culverhouse, Linda Owen, and Hedy Leutner. To all of them, I give my undying gratitude.

I am also grateful to Christy Ottaviano, the perfect editor, for her intelligence, farsightedness, and unwavering commitment to this book. Also thanks to Meredith Baldwin, who designed this book and created a stunning and sensitive cover and layout. In addition, I want to give a special thank-you to the many people who shared their personal experiences with me, including Midge Albert, Peter Amicucci, Camilla Boyer, Charisse Broome, Clyde Chamberlin, Aikaterini Chatzistyli, Ojoma Edeh, Rodger Fink,

Peg Holbrook, Barbara Horl, Marlise Johnson, Ishita Khemka, Barbara Kiefer, Lindsay Koehler, Pauline Manhertz, Mary Marcopul, Doug Marion, Joyce Miano, Alison Noble, Judy Reishtein, Ann Sparanese, Frances Treanor, Sandie Walters, Salifu Yamusah, and Aisha Zikria.

While doing my research, I received assistance from many informative people, including Roberta Halporn, executive director, The Center for Thanatology Research and Education, Brooklyn, New York; Murray Marks, co-director, Anthropology Research Center, University of Tennessee, Knoxville, Tennessee; Joan Huffman, trauma/surgical critical care physician, Lehigh Valley Hospital, Allentown, Pennsylvania; Bill Siegmann, curator for the arts of Africa and the Pacific Islands, Brooklyn Museum of Art, Brooklyn, New York; Donna Jones, editor, *MBNews*, Monument Builders of North America, Des Plaines, Illinois; Thomas Luke Conroy, superintendent, Oak Hill Cemetery, Nyack, New York; Leo and Debra Bodanski, superintendent and office manager, Brookside Cemetery, Englewood, New Jersey; Lisa Carlson, executive director, Funeral and Memorial Societies of America; George W. Clarke, National Selected Morticians, Northbrook, Illinois; George Lemke, executive director, Casket and Funeral Supply Association of America; Jack Springer, executive director, Cremation Association of North America; Nick Verrasto, *American Cemetery Magazine*, Iselin, New Jersey; Jennifer Songster, curator for audiovisuals, Ohio Historical Society, Columbus, Ohio; Miriam Bobkoff, reference librarian, Santa Fe Public Library, Santa Fe, New Mexico; Maja Keech, reference specialist, Prints and Photograph Division, Library of Congress, Washington, D.C.; and Pat Zimmermann, a teacher at the Smith School, Ramsey, New Jersey, and her sixth-grade class of 1996, who sent me their questions about corpses, coffins, and crypts.

Several people whom I have already thanked also carefully read all or part of my manuscript and offered helpful comments, including Roberta Halporn, Joan Huffman, and Thomas Conroy. In addition, I want to thank Dot Emer, a longtime children's librarian who now lives in Boca Raton, Florida, and Margaret Crocco, assistant professor of social studies and education, Teachers College, Columbia University, for their scrutiny and feedback.

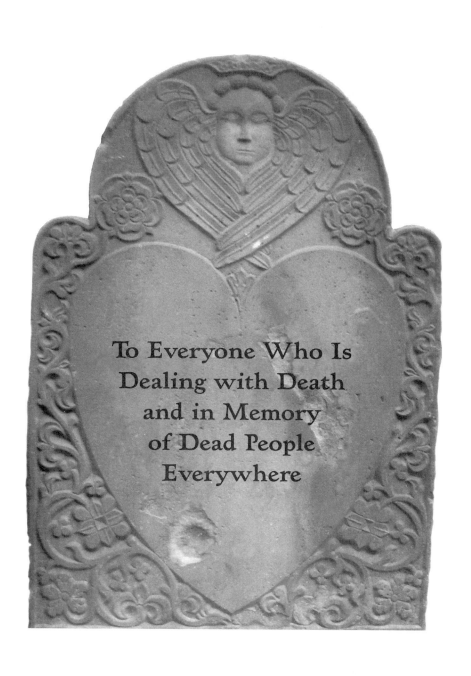

•Contents•

Corpses,
Coffins,
and Crypts

Preface

When Christy Ottaviano, an editor at Henry Holt, contacted me about writing this book, I experienced a tangle of emotions as different parts of me had different reactions: the creative part of me was challenged, the intellectual part was curious, and the emotional part was apprehensive. When I started to do some research about dead bodies and embalming, all of me felt queasy.

Surrounding my tangle of emotions was a sadness I still feel about the long-ago deaths of my brother and father. Jon was twenty when he died. I was twenty-one. Three years later my father died, two months after his fiftieth birthday. Now, I'm fifty-two and the sadness is mostly subliminal. However, it surfaces under certain circumstances. Christy's request turned out to be one of those circumstances, although she had no way of knowing that.

Christy also did not know that I have had a variety of experiences with corpses, coffins, and cemeteries. Once I spent a day in an apartment with my dead great-uncle's body. After he was cremated, his wife and I flew to Czechoslovakia (now the Czech Republic) to bury his cremated remains in the family plot in

Planting flowers on a grave is a common ritual, which is what I'm doing around my brother's gravestone in Randolph Center Cemetery in Randolph Center, Vermont. My father is buried beside Jon. A large marker with their last name, Morgan, is nearby.

Koryčany, remains that were in a box I carried on the airplane and put under my seat. Then there was my experience as a youngster when my father's friend Dr. Schwartz would come to our house with slices of people's brains in thick, narrow glass containers. Dr. Schwartz was doing research about the causes of mental illness, and he and my father, who was a psychiatrist, spent hours sitting at the kitchen table scrutinizing the brain slices for abnormalities. I remember being horrified that people's brains had been taken out of their bodies, although my father reassured me that the people were dead when their brains were removed and that they had agreed to let scientists study their brains after they died.

My mother, on the other hand, was interested in cemeteries. Occasionally I would find myself in a cemetery with her looking for graves. In particular, I remember the sweet spring smells and

Above: *David Colman and Linda Hickson standing outside the metal fence that encloses the family plot where Emily Dickinson is buried.*

warm sun of the day that we searched a cemetery until we found the poet Emily Dickinson's grave. It was raining when we went looking for the grave of Justin Morgan, a schoolteacher and owner of the original stallion of the breed of Morgan horses, but that didn't stop us—we just pretended that we were ducks.

At this point in my life, I haven't seen a brain slice in years, but I've continued visiting cemeteries. With my camera and notebook, I've traveled to cemeteries throughout the United States to photograph graves of historic women and to learn

Left: *It was a cold November day when David Colman, my son; Linda Hickson, a friend; and I went to visit Emily Dickinson's grave in West Cemetery, Amherst, Massachusetts. Although my mother had taken me to the grave when I was a child, I did not remember its exact location, so we split up and went looking. Happily it wasn't too long before I heard David shout, "Here she is!" Linda is copying down the inscription, which reads: "Emily Dickinson, Born Dec. 10, 1830; Called Back May 15, 1886." Previous visitors had left a rose, a stick, and a bundle of twigs on top of Dickinson's gravestone.*

Through my father and his father, I'm a descendant of Justin Morgan, a piece of my family history that came alive for me the first time I found his gravestone in Randolph Center Cemetery, and read the inscription. This is not his original gravestone but one that was erected at a later date. Some of my Morgan relatives are buried in the same cemetery, including my grandmother, "Grammie," my father, and my brother.

about the art, architecture, horticulture, and history that abound in many cemeteries.

My emotions and experiences may seem strange to some people. Or morbid. Or macabre. But most people aren't fazed. They accept my emotions and experiences in a matter-of-fact way. In addition they are prompted to start thinking about their own emotions and experiences with death. At least that is what I discovered when I was researching and writing this book. Ann Sparanese told me about her trip to the morgue: "I never knew that a dead body looked like that," she said. Barbara Horl recalled that she grew up next door to a crematorium. "I used to help my mother dust on Saturday mornings," she told me. "If

I discovered this sign for Moon Cemetery at the junction of two dirt roads in Madison County, Iowa. The cemetery was about a mile down the road.

the windowsill was particularly dusty, I'd say to my mother, 'I wonder who this is?' " Doug Marion told me about the six summers he spent working in a cemetery. "It was a wonderful job," he said. "There was always something interesting going on." Peg Holbrook wrote me a letter about a friend whose life and death hadn't been easy: "Her daughter and I were holding her hand at the end. When we buried her, her daughter put a teddy bear in the coffin, and I gave her a chocolate. I tried to put it under her hand, but it was really stiff, so I finally slipped it down by the lining. The kids put other stuff in the coffin too. She went out like an Egyptian queen down on her luck, which was, more or less, how she had lived."

Barbara Kiefer's husband, Major David Kiefer, a jet pilot who had flown in Vietnam, died when his jet plane crashed in 1976. After telling me about her husband's death, Barbara said, "I have a funny story to tell you. I have always been a champion shopper, someone who looks for a bargain. My friends and I are

A family tending to a new grave in a memorial park where all the graves have flat bronze markers. Pioneer Cemetery, Watsonville, California.

always trying to top each other. But when I got a used tombstone, I knew that no one could top that!" Barbara explained that because David was in the military, the United States government paid his funeral expenses, including the cost of a grave marker that would be placed flat on the ground. However, David's mother, Margaret Kiefer, was worried that the flat marker would get covered over with grass. According to Barbara, "We decided to add a piece of marble under the marker so that it would be elevated. But we didn't want to spend much money because we knew that David wouldn't want us to. So when the guy at the monument store said, 'I have an inscribed marble monument that was just returned because the people want a bigger one,' I bought it. We put the side with the inscription facedown on the ground and attached the plaque for David on top of it." Barbara told me her story with an infectious sense of humor and ended with the words: "We have to find some-thing to laugh about or life just gets too sad."

Before I actually start writing any book, I spend a lot of time thinking about how to present the factual material: how to make it irresistible, informative, and empowering. With this particular book, I added the challenge of how to minimize queasy feelings—my own and those of potential readers. At one point in my thinking, I realized that the factual material was irresistible, informative, empowering, and minimally queasy to me when I incorporated it with my own experiences and the experiences of people like Peg Holbrook and Doug Marion. So that is how I wrote this book, and, for example, why the chap-ter about what happens to dead bodies begins with Ann Sparanese's account of her trip to the morgue. I organized the material according to topics: defining death (Chapter 1), under-standing death (Chapter 2), what happens to dead bodies (Chapters 3, 4, and 5), where dead bodies end up (Chapter 6), burial rituals (Chapter 7), and death in the the arts and every-day life (Chapter 8). Of course the topics are connected and overlap, but each chapter has a particular emphasis. Although it was impossible to include all the available information about each topic, I tried to be as comprehensive as possible within the limits of this book. I also included people's last requests, a select list of burial sites, epitaphs, a guide to common carvings on gravestones, a chronology, a glossary, and a bibliography.

As for why I wrote this book: I wrote it because I believe that death, a hard, sad, unavoidable fact of life, is easier to accept

Christmas Tree with Thanksgiving Balloon on Graves. *Both Thanksgiving and Christmas are marked with these grave decorations—the wreaths on the gravestones and the Christmas tree with balls and tinsel. Tied to the tree is a plastic balloon with a scene of a cornucopia and the words* Happy Thanksgiving. *These graves are in Brookside Cemetery, Englewood, New Jersey. During my travels I've seen graves with pumpkins, oranges, fresh flowers, potted plants, birthday cards, and a variety of personal mementos. I've also seen people weeding, sweeping, praying, reading out loud, and crying. Thomas Luke Conroy, superintendent of Oak Hill Cemetery in Nyack, New York, told me about the young man who made repeated trips to the grave of his brother, who had died in a car crash. The anguished young man always came very late at night. Conroy, who lives in a house just inside the entrance to the cemetery, would go sit with the young man. "Sometimes he just cried. Sometimes he wanted to talk," says Conroy. One night the young man asked Conroy if he believed in hell. "This isn't the time to be worried about hell," Conroy told him. "Besides, even if there is a hell that doesn't mean anyone is in it."*

when we are able to talk about it and get answers to our questions. When we hear other people's stories. When we learn about the variety of attitudes and rituals that have existed concerning death and burials. Nobody is immune to death. People die. I will and so will you. But if we are prepared, we can deal with death, however and whenever it happens. That became clear to me in December 1980 when I received news that my grandmother had had a stroke. She was ninety-two years old and I was forty. I boarded a plane, rented a car, and followed a snowplow for hours to get to the hospital. I talked to myself while I drove. No denial, I said. She's dying. No heroics, I said. She abhors extraordinary lifesaving efforts. No games, I said. You won't see her again. No false cheer, I said. This is very sad. No maudlin sentimentality, I said. Grammie would hate that, and I smiled at the thought.

It was a crispy cold, bright afternoon when I arrived at the hospital. I parked the car and went inside. The door to my

Six pinwheels decorate a child's grave. The W in the bottom right-hand corner marks one corner of the Williamses' family plot in Randolph Center Cemetery, Randolph, Vermont, in which the child was buried.

grandmother's room was heavy as I pushed it open. "Hi, Grammie," I said as I stepped to the side of her bed and leaned over the metal railing. "It's Penny." Tears came to her eyes and a torrent of garbled words poured out of her mouth. But I couldn't understand her; the stroke had done too much damage. Finally she sagged, exhausted from the effort of trying to communicate with me. I didn't know what to do, but I knew that I had to do something. So I held her hands and told her stories about my children, her great-grandchildren, what they were doing, and how much they loved her. I reminisced about us, particularly about a memorable trip we had taken to Italy. I kept talking although Grammie seemed to be lost in another world.

Suddenly I heard a loud gurgling sound coming from her stomach. "Hey," I exclaimed, "listen to that, Grammie, your stomach is in a holiday mood!" I grinned and softly sang along with the cacophony from her insides, "Jingle bells, jingle bells . . ." For a moment the effects of the stroke disappeared. Grammie smiled, her eyes twinkled, and she laughed, her familiar merry laugh. The sound danced through me. My laughter joined hers like sleigh bells on a snowy, starry night. I hugged her, held her in my arms, then straightened up, put on my coat, and walked straightaway to the door. "Grammie," I said as I stopped and turned toward her, "I love you. This is probably the last time we'll see each other, but you will live inside me forever." The look on her face and the feeling inside me said it all. In the light of memories shared, love expressed, and good humor, death had become no more and no less than what it is— the physical end of our bodies.

Grammie died the next day. She couldn't be buried until the ground thawed in the spring, so her body remained in cold storage in the funeral home. Finally in June, I joined other family members and friends at the cemetery. The grave was dug. Grammie's coffin was there. My uncle gave a speech, my cousin sang, my sister-in-law read a poem, my mother and sister laid a bouquet of wildflowers on the coffin, and I read Scripture verses that Grammie had asked me to read. Then her coffin was lowered into the grave.

That is how we buried my grandmother. People with different religious beliefs would have done things differently. So would people from different cultures and geographic regions. And so have people throughout human history. The record of these various attitudes and practices is found in myths and legends, studies by anthropologists and archaeologists, oral histories, wills, epitaphs, art, music, literature, architecture, and burial places.

The Princeton Cemetery, Princeton, New Jersey.

It's an intriguing record. I hope that reading *Corpses, Coffins, and Crypts: A History of Burial* doesn't make you too queasy or tangle up your emotions too much. Instead, I hope that the book intrigues you and motivates you to think about how you will deal with death, an inevitable part of all our lives.

· one ·

Dead Is Dead:
Defining Death

My great-aunt Frieda Matousek called me with the news that her husband, Willi, was "having another attack." I wasn't surprised: Willi was eighty-six years old and he had several health problems, including heart disease.

"Call his doctor," I said. "I'm on my way."

When I arrived, Frieda met me at the door. "He's dead," she said. "Come see him."

I hugged her and kept my arm around her shoulders as we walked down the hallway to their bedroom. The bedroom was bright with sunshine and Willi lay stretched straight out on the double bed. Dressed in blue-and-white-striped pajamas, Willi's body was on top of the blankets, his head and shoulders were propped up by a pile of pillows, and his feet were bare. He looked exactly like Willi except that he was absolutely still and silent.

"Right after I talked to you, he made a noise, sat up a bit, and fell back," Frieda said. Just then the doorbell rang. I answered it.

"I'm the visiting nurse," the woman informed me. "I have an appointment to visit Mr. Willi Matousek."

"He's dead," I said. "He's in the bedroom."

"How do you know he's dead?" the nurse asked as she headed down the hallway.

This death certificate documents my brother's death. In many countries, including the United States, a death certificate is required in order to dispose of a body, settle an estate, make insurance claims, and get death benefits. The letters DOA mean Dead on Arrival.

This scene was repeated when the emergency medical technicians (EMTs) arrived at the door with all their equipment.

"He's dead," I said.

"How do you know?" they replied and rushed down the hall.

Then the police arrived.

"He's dead," I said.

"How do you know?" they replied.

At one level their question struck me as funny. "What do you mean, 'How do you know?'" I wanted to say. "He hasn't breathed or moved for at least an hour." But at another level I knew that just because Willi hadn't breathed or moved didn't necessarily mean that he was dead. Throughout history people have been declared dead when they really weren't.

In the late 1500s in England, Matthew Wall was thought to be dead until pallbearers accidentally dropped his coffin and he was revived. In the early 1600s in Scotland, Marjorie Elphinstone was supposedly dead until she groaned when grave robbers broke into her newly buried coffin to steal jewelry from her recently buried body. Forgetting about the jewelry, the robbers fled. Elphinstone climbed out of her coffin and walked home. In

Although this scene titled "Grave Robber Flees from a Corpse That Has Come to Life" was originally published in 1746, grave robbers were common in many times and places. In the case of Margaret Halcrow Erskine, a grave robber unintentionally saved her life. When Erskine appeared to have died in Chirnside, Scotland, in 1674, the sexton buried her in a shallow grave so that he could return at night and steal her jewelry. However, Erskine revived as the sexton was cutting off her finger to remove her ring. Although there's no information about what happened to the sexton, Erskine lived a long and productive life.

the 1860s passersby heard tapping coming from Philomèle Jonetre's grave. On exhuming her body, the director of the morgue in Paris saw her eyelids move. She revived but died the next day, really died. About the same time there was the case of a doctor who cut into a supposedly dead person only to have the person jump up and grab the doctor's throat. The "dead person" survived, but the doctor dropped dead of apoplexy. In the early 1900s a young girl had lain in her open coffin for thirty-six hours when a relative who happened to be a physician decided that she looked alive. He treated her and she recovered.

How can these mistakes happen? Experts have given various explanations for erroneous declarations of death and premature burials, including thanatomimesis, or death feigning; trances; narcotic overdose; concussion; syncope, or fainting; and asphyxia, or lack of oxygen. In 1884 a British medical journal, *Lancet,* offered this explanation: "It is not so much the undue haste as inexcusable carelessness that must be blamed for the premature burying of persons who are not really dead." In 1995 Dr. Kenneth V. Iserson wrote in his book *Death to Dust: What Happens to Dead Bodies?* that the words in *Lancet* "still ring true today," a dreadful thought for those of us still alive. Nevertheless, mistakes are extremely rare today.

The terror of premature burial has prompted people to devise various rituals and devices. Some ancient people waited until the dead body began to decay before they buried or cremated it. The Romans called out a person's name three times before putting the body on the funeral pyre. The ancient Jews stored

The Viele Memorial, West Point, Highland Falls, New York. *Egbert Ludovicus Viele, the man who designed this memorial for himself and his wife, was terrified of being buried alive. So he rigged up a buzzer system that would ring inside the cemetery caretaker's house if he found himself alive inside the memorial. The huge memorial is patterned after an ancient Egyptian pyramid, complete with two sphinxes, the symbol of the pharaoh, which was portrayed as a lion with a human head. When Viele died in 1902, his body was placed in a sarcophagus, or stone coffin, inside the memorial. The buzzer never rang, although one caretaker reported being seriously startled until he realized that what he thought was the buzzer was only the telephone. The buzzer is no longer connected.*

dead bodies in caves and open sepulchres and regularly checked on them for a period of time. Some people stuck pins under corpses' nails. One woman instructed her doctor to stick a long metal pin in her heart before she was actually buried. A man wanted a doctor "either to sever my head or extract my heart from my body, so as to prevent any possibility of the return of vitality." In 1896 the Association for the Prevention of Premature Burial was organized in England for people who wanted to have scientific tests performed on their corpses before they were buried.

In St. Helena's Episcopal Churchyard in Beaufort, South Carolina, there's a brick vault with the remains of a Dr. Perry. According to the church history, Dr. Perry was terrified of being buried alive. So he had his friends promise to bury him with a loaf of bread, a jug of water, and a pickax. He had his slaves build a brick vault aboveground with enough room for him to swing his ax. Perry was buried with the bread, water, and pickax. He must have been truly dead because the vault still remains intact.

In 1843 Christian Eisenbrandt of Baltimore, Maryland, filed a patent for a "new and useful improvement in coffins." Eisenbrandt's invention was a coffin rigged so that the lid would pop up if the occupant made the slightest movement. He described it as "a life-preserving coffin in case of doubtful death." Since Eisenbrandt's coffin worked only aboveground, other people developed devices that would detect signs of life underground. In Belgium, Count Karnicé-Karnicki invented a coffin that had a tube extending from the coffin to the surface of the ground. Any

Because she was terrified of flooding, P. Piedad L. F. De Ayala requested that she be buried in a coffin supported on columns in Key West City Cemetery, Key West, Florida. The end with her head was tilted upward. Undoubtedly, De Ayala knew about the hurricane of 1846 that flooded several cemeteries in Key West. According to one eyewitness, "The effects of the hurricane were terrible. The graveyard of this town . . . was entirely washed away, and the dead were scattered throughout the forest, many of them lodged in trees."

movement of the corpse's chest would activate a spring-loaded ball that was attached to the end of the tube in the coffin. A box with a flag, bell, and lamp was placed over the outside end of the tube. If the corpse activated the spring-loaded ball, the box lid opened to let light and air in the coffin, the flag appeared, the bell rang for a half hour, and the lamp lit up in the evening.

In the early 1900s in Germany, "waiting mortuaries" were built where bodies were stored until they started to decay, the only sure sign of death. Placed on slabs, bodies were covered with flowers from friends and relatives. According to one observer, "Many families have their dead photographed like this. . . . There is a room for the rich and another for the poor, adjoining each other. Nothing distinguishes them, except perhaps the quality of the flowers." A ring attached to a bell was placed on one of the corpse's fingers. If the corpse moved, the bell would ring and summon the round-the-clock attendant. Since corpses move as the putrefactive gases build up, bells rang all the time. According to one account, "The caretaker goes to ascertain the cause of the alarm, and, having assured himself that the corpse preserves all the signs of death, he readjusts the cord, and returns to continue his sleep." Attendants rarely found a living corpse, although on one occasion attendants found a five-year-old child "playing with the white roses which had been placed on its shroud."

As for Willi, he wasn't the type to worry about anything, especially not premature burial. "He is dead," the EMT finally said after carefully listening for a heartbeat with a stethoscope, feeling his carotid artery for a pulse, and checking his eyeballs for signs of responsiveness. Although Willi seemed to die suddenly, he hadn't. According to scientists, for Willi and everyone else death is a process. Willi's heart had stopped beating, but three hours after he died, his pupils still respond to a particular stimulus. His skin could still be a viable skin graft twenty-four hours after his death. Forty-eight hours after his death, his bones could still be a viable bone graft. Nevertheless, Willi as a functioning human being was past the point of no return. He was dead.

At different times in history, people have used a variety of methods for determining death, including using a feather or mirror to detect traces of breath. William Shakespeare describes the mirror method in his play *King Lear*, when he has Lear say,

Lend me a looking-glass;

If that her breath will mist or stain the stone,

Why, then she lives.

In colonial America some people believed that they could determine death this way: "Touch the flame of a candle to the tip of one of the great toes of the supposed corpse. A blister will raise. If life is gone, the blister will be full of air and will burst noisily when the flame is applied a few seconds more. If there is still life, the blister will not burst." In England a textbook published in 1817 offered these suggestions for determining that a person was really dead: "keeping the corpse warm under close watch for at least a week, with no indecent experiments for twenty-four hours except holding a looking-glass to the mouth or brushing the soles of the feet with strong pickle [because it is a strong acid]; or electricity; or warm baths; or pasting tissue-paper over the mouth and nose . . . If none of these seem conclusive, cut the jugulars, or separate the carotid arteries, divide the medulla, or pierce the heart."

In modern times the task of determining if a person is dead has become more complicated. Modern techniques and technology are used to revive and sustain people. Machines can keep a person's heart beating and blood circulating. These modern techniques and technologies have saved lives, including those of people whose brains no longer function, who are called brain-dead. This has forced people to figure out how to define and determine death in a new way. Today the most widely accepted definition is "death by whole brain criteria," which

An artist painted this deathbed scene in Europe in the late six- teenth century, depicting the battle for the dying man's soul being waged by the angels in one window and the devil in the other. As was typical of the time, there are many peo- ple around the dying person, a reflection of the medieval cus- tom that anyone could enter a dying person's room, including children.

means complete loss of function in the neocortex—the part of the brain that contains thoughts, perceives pain and pleasure, and controls voluntary actions—and in the brainstem, which controls breathing, wakefulness, and blood pressure. It is the legal definition in much of the United States and in a growing number of other countries. In his book *Death to Dust*, Kenneth Iserson describes the steps physicians normally take to establish irreversible loss of function: "(1) determine the cause of coma; (2) decide that irremediable structural brain damage has occurred; (3) eliminate reversible cause of coma such as extremely low body temperature, drug intoxication or a severe chemical imbalance; and (4) demonstrate that all brainstem reflexes, including breathing, are absent."

My day with Willi's dead body ended when two men arrived with a stretcher. They wrapped his body in a bright yellow blan-

One Day the Dreary Old King of Death *is the title of this picture that was published in the early 1800s in England. The use of a skeleton or skull to represent death began in the Middle Ages in western Europe, when people became preoccupied with death as the plague killed huge numbers of people. Other symbols were used in other times and places. The butterfly was a symbol of death in ancient Greece because the Greeks believed that the soul left the body after death in the form of a butterfly. Stories in which the chameleon is associated with death are widespread in southern and eastern Africa.*

ket, put it in a black body bag, strapped it to the stretcher, and wheeled the stretcher down the hallway and out the door.

"There goes Willi," I said. Bubba, Frieda's best friend, who had just arrived, said, "It is God's will."

"No, it's not! Willi just got old. That's all," Frieda quickly responded.

"God's will," Bubba insisted as she made the sign of the cross on her chest.

"Old age!" Frieda repeated.

Frieda and Bubba were engaging in an ancient discussion: Why do people die? There are many ways to answer that question. There are biological and physiological answers. In his book *How We Die*, Dr. Sherman Nuland describes a death like Willi's: "It [the heart] was not getting enough oxygen; it was not getting enough oxygen because it was not getting enough hemoglobin, the blood-borne protein whose function is to carry the oxygen; it was not getting enough hemoglobin because it was not getting enough blood; it was not getting enough blood because the heart's nourishing vessels, the coronary arteries, were hardened and narrowed by a process called arteriosclerosis (literally hardening of the arteries)."

There are also answers to the question "Why do people die?" in legends and myths. A Zulu myth says that God sent

This statue of Gautama Buddha, the founder of Buddhism, is in the Long Men Caves outside Loyang, China. The Buddha taught that nothing is permanent: "The world is a passing phenomenon. We all belong to the world of time. Every written word, every carved stone, every painted picture, the structure of civilisation, every generation of man, vanishes away like the leaves and flowers of forgotten summers. What exists is changeable and what is not changeable does not exist."

Chameleon to tell people that they wouldn't die. Sometime later God sent Lizard to tell people that they would die. While Chameleon was walking slowly and eating fruit along the way, Lizard scurried along, delivered the message, and returned to God. By the time Chameleon arrived, people had accepted Lizard's message and nothing could be changed. According to a legend from the Fiji Islands, when the first man, the father of the human race, was being buried, a god walked by. Having never seen a grave before, the god asked people standing there what was happening. When they told him that their father had just been buried, the god said, "Do not bury him; dig up the body again." The people refused. "He has been dead for four days and smells," they said. The god begged them to dig him up. "I promise you that he will live again," he said. But the people refused. "By disobeying me, you have sealed your own fate," the god declared. "Had you dug up your ancestor, you would have found him alive, and you yourselves when you passed from this world would have been buried as bananas are for four days, after which you would have been dug up not rotten, but ripe. But now, as a punishment for your disobedience, you shall die and rot."

A Navajo legend offers another explanation: From the beginning, people wondered, "Will we live forever or die?" So Coyote decided to answer the question by throwing a stone into the water. If it floated, they would live; if it sank, they would die. When it sank, the Navajo people became angry until they listened to Coyote's wise words: 'If we all live and continue to increase as we have done in the past, the earth will be too small

to hold us, and there will be no room for the cornfields. It is better that each of us should live but a limited time on this earth,
then leave and make room for the children."

Frieda and Bubba didn't argue long about why Willi had
died. Bubba decided to go pray. Frieda and I changed the sheets
on the bed. Then we had a cup of tea. Finally Frieda said that
she was ready to go to sleep and that I should go home to my
family. As I drove home I kept thinking about the absolute
stillness of Willi's body, a stillness that I had never experienced
before.

"Dead is dead," I heard myself saying out loud. "Dead is dead."

·t w o·

Death Is Destiny: Understanding Death

My sister, Cam, was three years old when our brother Jon died and six years old when our father died. As a three-year-old, Cam didn't really understand that Jon's death was final. She kept waiting for him to appear. When we took her to the funeral home and explained that Jon was in the closed coffin—"Jon's box," we called it—she said, "Open it! Let him out! He wants to play with me." As a six-year-old, Cam understood that Dad's death was final.

Cam's reaction was not unusual, according to research done in Europe after World War II by Maria Nagy. A psychologist, Nagy asked 378 Hungarian children ranging in age from three to ten years old about their thoughts and feelings about death. The children, who nicknamed Nagy "Auntie Death," had discussions with Nagy and drew pictures. In addition the older children followed Nagy's request to "write down everything that comes to your mind about death." Nagy studied their responses and concluded that some children go through three stages in understanding death. The youngest children—age three to about five—tend to be curious about death and ask matter-of-

In many times and places, large numbers of children died and still die. Six young children in the Ellis family died between 1838 and 1849. This is one of two plaques on the Ellises' monument listing the names of their children. Rural Cemetery, Worcester, Massachusetts.

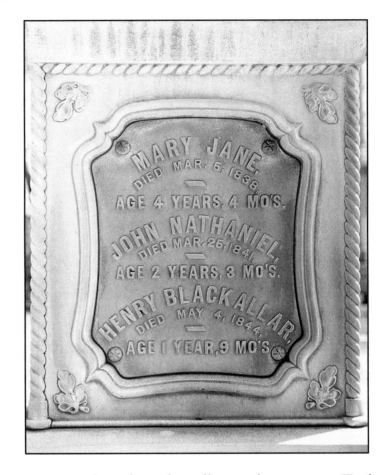

fact questions about funerals, coffins, and cemeteries. To them, death is a continuation of life but at a lower level: dead people can't see and hear as well as living people, they aren't quite as hungry, and they don't do very much. And they might return. Younger children appear to think that death is at best not much fun and boring and at the worst lonely and scary.

Beginning at about the age of five or six, children tend to realize that death is final and move into what Nagy named Stage 2. Although at this stage, many children realized that death was final, some of them thought that they could escape death if they were clever, careful, or lucky. Christy Ottaviano remembers thinking like that when she was in elementary school. "I had to walk past a cemetery to get to school," she recalls. "I thought that I wouldn't die if I held my breath the whole way. So I did until I was about nine or ten years old." Christy may have stopped because she moved into what Nagy identified as Stage 3 in understanding death. This is when children tend to realize that in addition to being final, death is also inevitable—everyone dies, even clever, careful, and lucky people. Or people who hold their breath when they walk past a cemetery. "Death is destiny," wrote one ten-year-old child. Another ten-year-old wrote, "Everyone has to die." According to Nagy, Stage 3, which starts at about age nine or ten, continues throughout life.

Nagy studied how a group of children in a modern western culture came to understand death. Prehistoric people struggled to understand death too. At least, that is what excavation of burial sites indicates. According to radiocarbon testing, some burial sites date back to 70,000 B.C.E. One site contained the remains of eleven people. Their legs were flexed and they lay on their backs, sides, or faces. A jawbone of a wild pig rested in the crook of one man's arm. Tools have been found in graves. So have bone pins, necklaces made from perforated shells, and bracelets. In many burials red ocher, a kind of earth, was sprinkled over the body and stag antlers were placed over the heads of the buried people. Many graves were collective, or graves where dead people were buried on top of each other. When the site filled up, it was covered with a stone slab or heap of stones.

By studying this evidence in burial sites, scientists have tried to figure out how prehistoric people understood death. For example, some scientists think that prehistoric people believed that life continued after death because they buried dead people with food, tools, and ornaments. Other scientists suggest that prehistoric people thought that red ocher symbolized blood and could be used to magically revitalize the corpse. There are several ideas about what it means that many corpses were buried with their legs flexed and lying on their sides. One idea is that this burial position resembles how a baby lies in the womb; therefore prehistoric people may have believed in rebirth. Since many of the legs and arms seemed tightly flexed as if they had

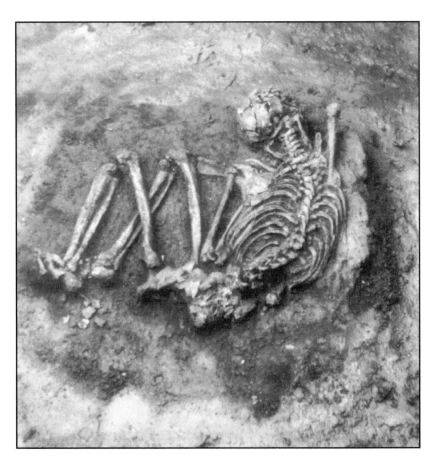

This ancient skeleton buried in a flexed position was uncovered during excavations of a Hopewell Indian burial mound in Ohio.

been bound, another idea is that perhaps prehistoric people feared death and bound dead people to ensure that they stayed put. Another explanation is simply that it was much easier for prehistoric people with their primitive tools to dig a grave for a body that was folded up and tightly bound.

Although we don't know exactly what the evidence in prehistoric burial sites means, it does tell us that from the beginning of human existence people have developed ways to understand death. Ancient people who lived in Mesopotamia believed that death was miserable. Being dead meant a grim existence in *kur-nu-gi-a*, "the land of no return," where dead people "live in darkness, eat clay, and are clothed like birds with wings." There was no alternative. Dead people were feared. Unless they were properly buried, they could cause all kinds of damage and disease. They might even eat the living. Ancient Egyptians had a very different understanding of death. As expressed in the myth of Osiris, an ancient Egyptian god who was killed by his evil brother, Set, and restored to life by his wife, Isis, the Egyptians believed in a god who granted immortality. They also believed that people's fates after death depended on how they lived their lives. Ancient Egyptians paid a lot of attention to death and developed elaborate rituals to ensure a happy afterlife.

Other people have understood death as a great cycle of death and rebirth, including the Tlingit Indians, who lived on the northwest coast of North America before the Europeans arrived. According to the Tlingits, people were born, died, and incarnated again as babies in a never-ending cycle, just as the salmon that they depended on came each summer and left each

This is the mummy mask of Tutankhamen, a king of ancient Egypt. Tutankhamen's royal tomb, discovered in 1922, contained everything he would need to enjoy life in the next world, including his sandals, furniture, and food. The mask was made of beaten gold and covered the head and shoulders of the mummy. It was inlaid with lapis lazuli, feldspar, carnelian, calcite, obsidian, and polychrome glass. Scientists compared it with the mummy and concluded that it is a life-size and lifelike portrait of the king, who was about eighteen years old when he died.

winter. Hindus and Buddhists understand death as a cycle of death and rebirth too, although in different ways from the Tlingits and from each other. For the Hindus the soul, or real self, of the person is eternal but must be reincarnated in different forms until it ultimately attains *moksha,* or spiritual and physical liberation. According to the *Upanishads,* ancient Hindu scriptures,

As a goldsmith, taking a piece of gold, transforms it into another newer and more beautiful form, even so this self, casting off this body and dissolving its ignorance, makes for itself another newer and more beautiful form like that of the ancestors or of the heavenly musicians, of the gods of Prajapati, of Brahma or of other creatures.

For the Buddhist the soul changes and is reincarnated until it frees itself from being attached to anything. In his essay *The Death That Ends Death in Hinduism and Buddhism*, L. Bruce Long writes, "The soul . . . can achieve total and eternal cessation of rebirth together with the peace of Nirvana by realizing that all things . . . are illusory, insubstantial and transitory." According to Dogen, the famous Zen master, "In life there is nothing more than life, in death nothing more than death: we are being born and dying at every moment."

The belief that life, in one way or another, continues after death is perhaps the most common understanding of death. Some people believe that dead people may take on another form like vampires or ghosts. Or they go to a different place. According to ancient Hebrews, people might end up in Sheol, or "the Pit." In the book of Job in the Old Testament, Sheol is described as "the land of gloom and deep darkness, the land of gloom and chaos, where light is as darkness." In the book of Isaiah, a person who "is brought down to Sheol" will discover that "maggots are the bed beneath you, and worms are your covering." Other people have believed in other places: the ancient Minoans believed in Elysium, a blissful place; the ancient Greeks believed in Hades, a miserable place; and the Scandinavians believed in Valhalla, a place where men who were killed in battle were escorted by Valkyries, or warrior-maids, to fight all day and feast all night.

Many religious people, including Jews, Christians, and Muslims, believe that dead people come to life again with God. For Jews the time comes when the Messiah comes, but only people who have lived good lives will get to be with God. Christians believe that Jesus Christ, as God in human form, was raised from the dead so that his followers could be too. At one time in Ireland, it was the custom for Christians to remove the nails from the coffin before it was lowered in the grave so that the dead person could speedily arise to heaven when the time came. Muslims believe that when the last, or judgment, day comes, everyone, dead or alive at the time, will be judged by God. A person goes to heaven if the book in which angels have

This grave in Mt. Olivet Cemetery in Washington, D.C., is covered with seashells, a tradition brought to America by enslaved Africans. Some people believed the seashell held the dead person's soul, which lived forever.

هو

اللہ لا اله الا هو الحی القیوم

GOD THERE IS NO GOD BUT HIM,
THE LIVING, THE ETERNAL ONE.

بسم الله الرحمن الرحیم

IN THE NAME OF GOD, THE COMPASSIONATE, THE MERCIFUL

بلی من اسلم وجهه لله وهو محسن فله اجر عند ربه ولا خوف علیهم ولا هم یحزنون

INDEED, THOSE THAT SURRENDER THEMSELVES TO GOD AND DO GOOD WORKS
SHALL BE REWARDED BY THEIR LORD; THEY SHALL HAVE NOTHING TO FEAR OR TO REGRET.

ان الذین قالوا ربنا الله ثم استقاموا فلا خوف علیهم ولا هم یحزنون

THOSE THAT SAY: OUR CREATOR IS GOD, AND FOLLOW THE STRAIGHT PATH
SHALL HAVE NOTHING TO FEAR OR TO REGRET

اولئک اصحاب الجنة خالدین فیها جزاء بما کانوا یعملون

THEY SHALL FOREVER DWELL IN PARADISE AS A REWARD FOR THEIR LABOURS.

THE KORAN

Muslim Woman's Grave. *In order to be ready when the final judgment day comes, a Muslim must be buried facing Mecca, the most holy city of Islam. Because the graves in Oak Hill Cemetery in Nyack, New York, don't face directly east, a Muslim who wanted to bury his mother there bought several plots and had this grave dug diagonally across them so that it faced east toward Mecca. According to Thomas Luke Conroy, superintendent of Oak Hill Cemetery, the woman was buried on the same day that she died in a plain pine coffin. After the prayers were said, the coffin was lowered into the grave. Then the eldest son climbed down a ladder that Conroy had provided; opened the coffin; turned his mother's body, which was dressed in a white shroud, over on her side so that her face was toward the east; closed the coffin; and climbed out of the grave. The ladder was removed, and the family helped fill the grave with dirt. The verse from the Koran is inscribed on the gravestone in three languages: Arabic, Farsi, and English.*

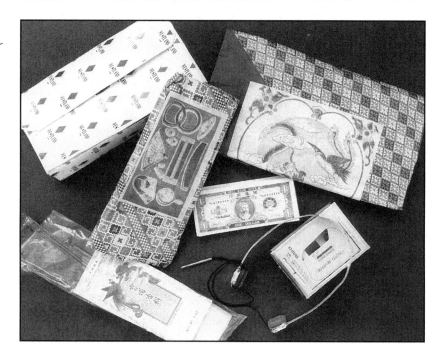

In the United States today, burning paper goods is an integral part of many Chinese funerals and the Ch'ing Ming Festival, which is celebrated during the first week in April. This is a photograph of some items that are burned for the spirit's use in the afterlife: a purse, a folded man's robe, a folded woman's robe, paper replicas of money that in America is called a "Bank of Hell" note, a Walkman, and a package of incense.

recorded their good and bad deeds is placed in that person's right hand. If it is put in the left hand, the person goes to hell.

Many people believe that dead people continue to live as ancestors and that living and dead people can communicate. They also believe that the activities of the dead in the next world can bring good fortune to the living people, assuming that the living continue to honor and provide for the dead. In ancient China shelves were set in the wall of the house to hold the wooden tablets that were inscribed with the ancestor's name and title. On certain dates incense would be burned and candles lit in front of the tablets. Food would be offered on festive occasions, and the family would worship before the tablet and kowtow, or kneel and touch their foreheads to the ground to show profound respect. During the Ch'ing Ming, or First Feast of the Dead at Spring Festival time, the graves were swept and the

The photograph of the grave in Cypress Hill Cemetery in Brooklyn, New York, shows the can in which paper goods were burned lying on its side. The wooden tablet is used to mark a grave before the monument is ready to be erected. It contains the name of the deceased person and information about her or his genealogy.

ancestor's needs for money, food, and clothing were provided for through rituals that included burning paper money.

When my son David was an exchange student in Nigeria, he lived for a time in a Yoruba village in southwest Nigeria. According to David, "Soon after I arrived, I noticed two graves beside the house where I was staying. The graves were side by side, with one grave flush against the wall of the house. They were two long slabs of cement raised above the ground about eight inches. It was the grandparents of the family who lived in

These gravestones reflect how ideas about death changed in the northeastern part of the United States from the 1600s to the 1800s. Top left: The skull, also called the "death's-head"; crossbones; hourglass; and flames symbolized the strict Puritan doctrine of death, sin, and damnation. Although it is rare to see these symbols together, it is common to see at least one, particularly the skull, on gravestones from the 1600s and early 1700s. Top right: By the late 1720s, a new emphasis on resurrection was reflected as wings, and the symbol was added to the skulls. Bottom left: By the end of the 1700s, the skull was replaced by the cherub as a metaphor for the soul. Bottom right: By the 1800s, many people understood death as an inevitable part of nature. They focused more on grief than on resurrection, and symbols of mourning, such as this weeping willow, became popular. In addition to changes in symbols, it is common to see changes in written language on old gravestones, which is why Hannah "lyeth," Mary "lyes." On old gravestones, the y with a small e for a hat is an abbreviation for the word the. First Presbyterian Church Burial Ground, Elizabeth, New Jersey.

the house. My Nigerian friend Yemi Tinuoye explained that the Yoruba people believe that after people die, they become ancestors, who are the highest elders. So the family buried their relatives in their living compound because they wanted their ancestors nearby in order to share good and bad news and ask them for advice."

Although many people learn how to understand death from their culture and families, other people don't, or they learn things that don't make sense to them. For people who are trying to understand death or who are just curious, there are many books to read, including religious ones such as the Koran, the sacred scripture of Islam; the Bible, the collection of sacred books of Judaism and Christianity; the Vedas, sacred texts that are basic to Hinduism; and *The Tibetan Book of the Dead*, which contains various Buddhist teachings about "how to die well." There's also a huge amount of other material—secular books, magazine articles, pamphlets, audiotapes, and videos. And there are people in our own lives who have experience and insights. When her mother died, Sandie Walters, a high school teacher, learned a lot from her students. "My students wrote me wise and touching notes on a sympathy card," Sandie told me. Then she showed me the card and read out loud the words that a student named Cachet had written: "I'm not going to say I know how you feel, but when my mother passed away, I cried and cried and cried until I realized that it wasn't going to bring her back. So I just talk to her every night and continue on with my life."

A "Tellem" figure of the Dogon people in the Republic of Mali that was most likely used to venerate ancestors in funerary rites, specifically to petition for rain.

When Pat Zimmermann saw this picture, she said, "That could be me or any member of my family standing by my father's grave." Princeton Cemetery, Princeton, New Jersey.

Understanding death doesn't necessarily take away our anxieties or fears about our own death or our sadness about other people's deaths. But it does help us find ways to continue on with our lives. That's what Cachet discovered. It's also what I've discovered.

·three·

What Happens to Corpses: Decomposition, Transplants, Autopsies, and Embalming

"I didn't really want to go into the viewing room with Janet. But she was getting upset by then, jittery. So I went," recalled Ann Sparanese about her trip to the morgue. Janet's son, Bill, had been missing for several days when the police called to say they had found a car registered to Bill. On the nearby beach, they had found a body. Janet told Ann that she had no doubt that it was Bill's body, but that she had to identify it officially at the morgue. According to Ann, "Janet was calm. She asked if I would drive her because she had to drive Bill's car back."

A police officer met Ann and Janet. He explained that he would take them into a room to view the body. He stressed that there would be a partition of glass between them and the body. According to Ann, "The room was small, no furniture, just a partition with a big window. On the other side of the window was a table with a body on it. The body was covered; just the face was showing. I stayed back a few steps, but Janet moved up close to the glass. 'Yes, that's Bill,' she said. Then we left. Janet was very stoic."

Bill had committed suicide. By the time his body was discovered, it had started to decompose. "I had seen dead bodies before,
but they were the fixed-up ones on display at funeral homes,"
Ann said. "The sight of Bill's body took my breath away. His features were almost indistinguishable. It was horrifying to see the
decomposing corpse of someone who I thought was a great guy."

For me Ann's story was particularly painful and poignant
because my brother's body had started to decompose before it
was discovered. A maid had found Jon's body in a hotel room
several days after he died of viral pneumonia. He had left college a few days before spring vacation to make a surprise visit to
his girlfriend. Sick with what he thought was a bad cold, Jon
had gone to the college infirmary. Not realizing how sick he
was, the staff told him that he was well enough to travel.
Although I never saw Jon's body, my older brother identified it
in the morgue, and his descriptions were as gruesome as Ann's.
I was haunted by the images until I realized that everyone's
body—Bill's, Jon's, eventually mine—decomposes. "The physi-
cality of a human corpse is undeniable. It is a carcass, with a pre-
disposition to decay, to become noisome, obnoxious to the
senses, and harrowing to the emotions," says Joseph Carr, former chief of pathology at San Francisco General Hospital.

In his book *Death to Dust*, Kenneth Iserson describes part of
the process of decomposition: "Once the heart stops beating,
the blood begins to settle in the parts of the body that are the
closest to the ground, usually the buttocks and back when the
corpse is supine. The skin, normally pink-colored by the oxy-
gen-laden blood in the capillaries, becomes pale as the blood

drains out into the large veins." Livor mortis, or purple-red discoloration of the skin, appears within minutes to hours. After completely relaxing at the moment of death, the muscles stiffen into what is known as rigor mortis, which begins within two to six hours of death. Eyelids, neck, and jaw are affected first. Other muscles and internal organs such as the heart are affected during the next four to six hours. Rigor mortis lasts for twenty-four to eighty-four hours, until the muscles relax and become flaccid. During this time the body cools.

About the second or third day after death, putrefaction, or decay, begins. As gruesome as it is, the signs of putrefaction—greenish skin discoloration and putrid odor—were considered

This drawing of Le Morgue, or the morgue, originally appeared in a book published in Paris in 1840. The first morgue in Paris was a vacant butcher shop, where people came to identify bodies of missing relatives and friends. In the picture the woman with the uplifted arms has apparently recognized the corpse on the stretcher.

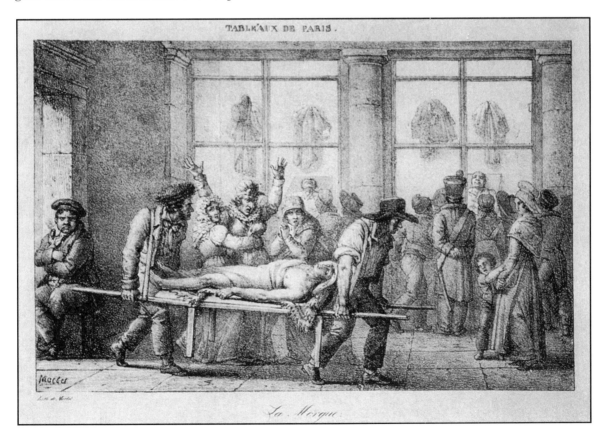

reassuring in many cultures because it meant that a person was truly dead. In ancient times the Greeks and Etruscans painted an important god the color that they used to represent rotting flesh—aquamarine. The putrefaction process progresses step by step: the skin loosens . . . eyes bulge out . . . bloody fluids seep out. . . . Then, according to Iserson, "After three to four weeks, the hair, nails, and teeth loosen and the grossly swollen internal organs begin to rupture and eventually liquefy."

In time a corpse dries out and only the bones remain, although many factors affect the length of time the process takes. Left outside in warm or hot weather, an adult corpse typically becomes a skeleton in two to four weeks. Burying an adult corpse without a coffin in a shallow grave, one to two feet deep, will stretch out the process to a few months or a year. An adult corpse without a coffin buried six feet deep will usually take five to ten years to turn into a skeleton. In places such as Scotland and the North Sea island of Amrum, where graves were reused, bodies that were buried in wooden coffins were typically left undisturbed for twenty to thirty years before a new corpse was buried in the same grave. In the United States some people think that they can stop decay by having a corpse embalmed and buried in a metal airtight casket, but the corpse still decomposes; it just takes longer, depending on a variety of factors. "Given enough time even the bones will disappear," Dr. Murray Marks, co-director of the Anthropology Research Center, University of Tennessee, told me. "The body does go back to nature."

Decomposition is just one of the things that can happen to

The two skeletons on Ruth Carter's headstone in The Granary cemetery in Boston, Massachusetts, were carved in the late 1600s by a stone-carver who signed his initials, "J.N." According to Harriette Merrifield Forbes, one of the earliest photographers of gravestones in New England, "The stone of Ruth Carter . . . has a very new and very startling feature— two skeletons. . . . Ordinarily one sufficed. Perhaps one of these depicts her as she lay in her coffin; the other, walking away with a raised hand and a jaunty air as if, freed from confinement, she was going forth for new life and new work. Probably the boxes on which these skeletons stand represent the coffin. The lily springing from the vase with its wealth of foliage may be simply ornamental or it may symbolize the glorified Ruth blooming in the Garden of God."

corpses. They can also serve as treasure troves. For example, tissues and organs can be transplanted from dead people to living people. At least twenty-five different types of tissue and organs can be used for transplants. Iserson lists some of them: "skin to help seriously burned patients cover and protect their wounds from infection and fluid loss; corneas [lenses of the eye] to allow those whose eyes are clouded or deformed to see again; bone and cartilage transplants to provide patients with a foundation on which their own bone may grow or to replace damaged joint tissues; temporal bones including inner ear structures to restore hearing to some who are deaf; heart valves to allow some patients' own hearts to function correctly; and veins to permit others to have coronary artery bypass surgery."

While I was writing this book, I saw a bumper sticker that read: "Don't take your organs to heaven. Heaven knows we need them here." In the United States, organ donations are governed by the Uniform Anatomical Gift Act, which has been adopted by every state with slight variations. People who qualify under the law can sign a Uniform Donor Card, which includes information about what the person is willing to donate. Organ and tissue donations are endorsed by most major religions. However, Muslims, Orthodox Jews, Rastafarians, Shin-

I spotted this billboard with a message about organ and tissue donations in southern California.

tos, and Zoroastrians typically oppose donations. According to Shinto, Japan's state religion, making donations hurts the *shitai*, or corpse, and thus the *itai*, or soul of the dead person, and that could cause misfortune for the family.

Corpses are also a rich source of information. Homicide detectives and forensic pathologists study corpses to find clues in murder cases. Forensic entomologists find clues by studying the insects on the corpse. Insects detect the odor of a newly dead body long before people do. Flies, especially flesh flies and blowflies, arrive first from as far away as two miles and lay thousands of eggs that soon hatch maggots. Then come beetles, spiders, mites, and millipedes. "Not only do insects swarm over an exposed corpse in great numbers, but they also arrive in a very precise sequence depending upon the body's location and condition," Iserson writes. "Since the exact feeding pattern varies with a body's location, the time of death, and the climate, forensic entomologists are often able to determine the date of death very accurately—even a decade later."

In Tacoma, Washington, entomological investigators identified two generations of maggots on the body of a man found dead of a gunshot wound. Since a generation of maggots generally reaches adulthood in three weeks, the investigators were able to determine the date of the man's death. With that information they discovered that the victim had been at a party where another man fired a gun and accidentally killed him. Partygoers had moved the victim's body in an attempt to delay and confuse the police.

Medical students dissect corpses in order to learn about the

Body Snatching. *First published in the early 1660s in the Netherlands, this picture depicts a common occurrence—body snatching. In different times and different places, people have stolen bodies from graves for a variety of reasons. In ancient Rome dead baby parts were stolen and used for recipes in witchcraft and sorcery. Corpses have been kidnapped for ransom money. Until the late nineteenth century, there were few, if any, legal ways that medical schools in Europe and the United States could acquire corpses for anatomical studies. So professional body snatchers regularly stole corpses and sold them to medical schools. For their own personal use medical students and physicians stole corpses too. Body snatching still occurs today, although it is no longer common.*

human body and to practice surgical procedures. Scientists examine corpses to get information about effects of diseases and the usefulness of certain treatments. Much of the information comes from an autopsy, or medical examination of a corpse, that is performed by a pathologist, or medical doctor who has special training in anatomy. In his book *How We Die*, Dr. Sherwin B. Nuland writes, "Together, pathologist and newly deceased patient undertake the obligation promised by the time-honored avowal that stares down on them from plaques on the walls of hundreds of autopsy rooms all over the world: *Hic est locus ubi mors gaudet succurso vitae*—'This is the place where death rejoices to come to the aid of life.'"

In dissecting a body, first the pathologist usually makes a Y-shaped incision, one cut from each shoulder or armpit that meet at the bottom of the breastbone and continue as one incision down the middle of the abdomen to the area just above the genitals. After removing the front part of the ribs and breastbone, the pathologist examines the organs and their surrounding area. To examine the brain, the pathologist parts the hair, makes an incision behind the ears and across the scalp, and then pulls the front of the scalp over the face and the back of the scalp over the nape of the neck. Then the pathologist uses a high-speed saw to make an opening in the skull in order to examine the inside for signs of infection, swelling, injury, or deterioration. Next the pathologist removes, dissects, and examines the internal organs. Finally samples of tissues, fluids, and other specimens are sent to the laboratory for analysis. Throughout the process the pathologist takes notes, draws diagrams, and takes photographs and X rays, especially for forensic autopsies, or an autopsy that is performed when a death is connected to a crime.

Although autopsies are invaluable, they are also controversial. Of course, there are situations when people don't have a choice and autopsies are required for legal reasons. When given a chance, however, many people refuse to give permission to have an autopsy performed. Some people can't bear the thought of having their dead body, or their loved one's body, cut open and probed by "strangers." Other people reject autopsies for religious reasons. In the United States, many people want the corpse to remain intact so that it can be embalmed, or preserved with chemicals, and fixed up for people to view. However, the fact is that pathologists can perform an autopsy in a way that doesn't prevent the corpse from being embalmed and viewed.

Embalming is a very old practice. The ancient Babylonians, Sumerians, and Greeks coated corpses with oils, spices, and perfumed unguents, or salves. Bodies were pickled in vinegar. When Alexander the Great, king of Macedonia and conqueror of the Persian Empire, died during a military expedition, his body was supposedly immersed in honey to preserve it for the trip back to Greece. After Lord Nelson, a famous British admiral, was killed, his body was said to have been shipped back to England in a cask of brandy. During the voyage, the sailors used pieces of macaroni as straws to sip brandy from the cask, apparently the origin of the expression "tapping the Admiral," which is still used by British sailors in reference to getting a drink of brandy.

Other types of embalming do more than retard decay; they stop it and preserve the corpse to some extent. Mummies, or

corpses whose skin is preserved over the skeleton, are the best-known example. Nature creates some mummies. For example, bodies left in hot deserts dehydrate, or dry out, instead of decomposing and mummify naturally. In arctic regions bodies can freeze and never decompose. In 1996 the mummified body of an Inca girl was discovered entombed in the ice on 20,700-foot Mount Ampato, near Arequipa, Peru. Mummies have been found in certain bogs in northern European countries, including Denmark, Germany, and Holland. Known as "bog people," the corpses were naturally mummified by the humic and tannic acids in the bog's soil.

Other mummies have been created by human beings. The ancient Egyptians created the first human-made mummies because they believed that the soul left the body at the time of death but rejoined it in the next world. Therefore the body had to be preserved in such a way that the soul would recognize it. The Egyptian art of embalming developed over many years. According to Herodotus, an ancient Greek historian who visited Egypt, there were three different procedures for turning three types of dead people—the rich, not-so-rich, and poor—into mummies. For the rich, Herodotus described a complex process of removing everything inside the corpse except the heart, which the mummy would need in the next world; washing the corpse with palm wine and spices; and covering it with natron, a natural salt, for seventy days. In addition the corpse would be rubbed with a mixture of cedar oil, wax, natron, and gum; stuffed with wads of linen, sand, or sawdust; and wrapped in layers of linen bandages. The not-so-rich process was more streamlined. As for the poor, Herodotus reported that the process was simply "to clear out the intestine with a clyster [or flush it] and let the body lie in natron the seventy days, after which it is at once given to those who come to fetch it away."

Embalming was practiced in other cultures too. Archaeologists have found evidence that the prehistoric Paraca Indians, who lived in what is now known as Peru, used sophisticated embalming techniques. So did the Guanche, who removed the viscera, dried the body, and stuffed it with salt and plants. In 1770 one thousand mummies were discovered in a cave on Tenerife, one of the Canary Islands where the Guanche had lived. In Japan huge candles were used to smoke dry the corpses of certain Buddhist priests in order to venerate them. In other cultures, however, embalming was seldom if ever practiced. The ancient Jews and early Christians viewed embalming as a pagan practice, although some notable Jews and Christians were embalmed. According to the Bible, Joseph and his father were embalmed. Upon his death in 814, Charlemagne, founder of the Holy Roman Empire, was embalmed, dressed in elegant clothes, and placed in a sitting position in his tomb at Aachen. In 1995 Mary Marcopul had the experience of visiting St. Mark's Syrian Orthodox Cathedral in Teaneck, New Jersey, and seeing the embalmed, seated body of Archbishop Athanasius Y. Samuel, the highest-ranking leader of the church in the United States and Canada. "I had just stopped to see the inside of the cathedral. I didn't know that Archbishop Samuel's body was there," Mary told me. "When I saw him dressed in his elaborate vestments, seated in a chair in the chancel, I was afraid. But then I saw other people going up and paying their respects, and I thought I should too. So I started walking up to him. I'd walk a bit, then sit in a pew, then walk. Finally I got close enough to see that he had the most amazing, peaceful expression on his face, and I wasn't afraid anymore." Other religious groups, including Sikhs, Muslims, Jews, Buddhists, and Hindus, typically either discourage or outright prohibit embalming.

Today embalming is primarily practiced in the United States, and the most commonly used method is arterial embalming. Rodger Fink got a glimpse of the process through the window of his auto-body shop. "My shop is behind a funeral home. Once they left the back door open, and I saw a metal table with a body strapped to it tipped up vertically so that the head was pointed toward the floor," he told me. Then he put his fingers where his neck joins his shoulders and made a cutting motion. "The guy who works there told me that's how they get the blood out and put the embalming fluid in." According to Kenneth Iserson, "The embalmers select large arteries and veins, expose them, and then insert the hollow metal tubes they will use to inject chemicals and aspirate blood and fluids."

The blood and fluids drain into a gutter in the floor. From the gutter, the blood and fluids commonly go into the sewer or a pail that is emptied into the sewer. While the blood is draining out of a large vein, the embalmer is injecting three or four gallons of a chemical solution that is mostly formaldehyde and methyl (wood) alcohol into a large artery. Before draining and injecting the corpse, the embalmer performs a series of steps, including disinfecting the corpse, securing the eyes and mouth in a closed position, and putting tight-fitting plastic clothing on the body to contain any leaking embalming fluid and undrained body fluid.

After being embalmed, a corpse undergoes a detailed makeup process so that it resembles as closely as possible the appearance of the person who has died. To give color to the face and hands, the embalmer can choose from cosmetics with names that range from Black, Caucasian, Spanish Olive, and Japanese to Outdoor Natural, Healthy Old Age, and Sallow Old Age. Finally the corpse is typically dressed in clothing that the family provides, such as a new suit or dress, a favorite outfit, or a uniform. When Linda Hickson was a little girl, she remembers her grandmother showing her a black crepe dress that was hanging in her closet and saying, "That's the dress I want to be laid out in." In her book *The American Way of Death*, a 1963 exposé of the American funeral industry, Jessica Mitford describes the whole process as a body being "sprayed, sliced, pierced, pickled, trussed, trimmed, creamed, waxed, painted, rouged and neatly dressed."

Embalming became popular in the United States during the Civil War. Prior to that time, ice was typically used to retard decomposition until a corpse was buried, although a few undertakers were practicing and improving embalming techniques. When thousands of men started dying on the battlefields, some undertakers set up business nearby. As the carnage continued, the government agreed to pay for embalming the bodies of soldiers that were shipped home. By the end of the war, approximately thirty thousand to forty thousand dead soldiers were embalmed, as was President Abraham Lincoln's body after he was assassinated. Before Lincoln was buried in Springfield, Illinois, his body was displayed in an open coffin in Washington, D.C., New York, and Chicago, providing a showcase for the burgeoning embalming business. "I saw him in his coffin," wrote one observer. "The face was the same as in life. Death had not changed the kindly countenance in any line."

Although embalming was originally promoted as a way to preserve corpses, by the 1880s it was being advertised as a necessity to protect people from disease. From that time to this, many

scientists have challenged that claim. Nevertheless, the funeral industry has continued to promote embalming, even on the Internet, where the National Funeral Directors Association claims on its Web site that embalming is "for the public health." According to Lisa Carlson, a critic of embalming and executive director of the Funeral and Memorial Societies of America, "That's a totally erroneous notion. Modern embalming techniques are themselves a public health hazard. For example, body fluids go into the common sewer, followed by a splash of Clorox." Despite the controversy, embalming remains popular in America because it makes it possible to fix up the body and keep it laid out in an open coffin for two to three days so that friends and relatives can view the body of the dead person at a wake. Typically people walk up to the coffin, look at the person who has died, and pray or meditate about what the dead person has meant to them. Embalming is also widespread because many people believe that it is required by law, although that is not generally true in the United States unless a body is transported across state lines.

Natural decomposition, transplants, autopsies, and embalming aren't the only things that can happen to corpses. There are still more common and uncommon things that can happen.

Opposite: A Civil War surgeon is standing behind the body of a dead soldier that he is embalming. The soldier is stretched out on a door—note the hinge on the back of the left-hand side—that is resting on two barrels. Although Civil War corpses were frequently embalmed outside, most corpses, even as late as the 1950s, were embalmed at home. The embalmer would arrive with a device that was used to cool the body, known as a "table-cooling board," set it up, get to work, and pour all the fluids from the embalming process down the sink.

·four·

Bones and Ashes: Cremation and Other Ways to Dispose of Corpses

About a week after Willi died, Frieda called to tell me that Willi was ready to be "picked up." Together we went to the funeral home. After a short wait, an attendant handed us a small cardboard box wrapped in brown paper. Frieda took it, put it in her cloth shopping bag, and we walked back to her apartment. In the living room, Frieda took the package out of her shopping bag, opened it, and removed a small urn that held what was left of Willi after he had been cremated—less than ten pounds of bone fragments. "Willi, you're home now," Frieda said as she carefully put the urn on the coffee table in her living room.

Willi's body was cremated in a crematorium, a specially designed furnace. The crematory operator had placed his body in a wood coffin, slid it into the cremation chamber, and turned on a fire that could heat up to 2,500 degrees. First the coffin burned and then the body, which, like every human body, contained water, carbon-based soft tissues, and bone. The intense heat evaporated the water, burned the soft tissues, and turned the bone into fragments. The whole process took between two and a half to three hours and yielded somewhere between six

and a half to nine pounds of bone fragments. Today most cremated remains are processed into smaller pieces. "They're put in a stainless steel bowl with a blade, like a Cuisinart," explained Jack Springer, executive director of the Cremation Association of North America. According to some state laws, cremated remains have to be processed to almost a powder if they're going to be scattered. Camilla Boyer, who helped scatter her brother's cremated remains, told me that they felt like talcum powder.

After observing the cremation of his mother's body, George Bernard Shaw, the famous English writer, wrote: "I went behind the scenes at the end of the service and saw the real thing. People are afraid to see it; but it is wonderful. I found there the violet coffin opposite another door, a real unmistakable furnace door. When it lifted there was a plain little chamber of cement and firebrick. . . . It looked cool, clean, sunny, though no sun could get there. . . . Then the violet coffin moved again and went in, feet first. And behold! The feet burst miraculously into streaming ribbons of garnet-colored lovely flame, smokeless and eager . . . and as the whole coffin passed in it sprang into flame all over; and my mother became that beautiful fire."

Prehistoric people practiced cremation, and by the early Stone Age it was commonly used in northern Europe and the Near East. During the next thousand years, cremation spread into the British Isles, Spain, Portugal, Hungary, northern Italy, and Greece. Around 600 B.C.E. cremation was adopted by the early Romans, and as the Roman Empire expanded, the practice of cremation spread. Jews, however, continued to practice their ancient tradition of inhumation, or in-ground burial. Several

Certificate of Cremation

North Bergen, N. J., ...MAY 12, 1975..........

Garden State Crematory

hereby certifies that the late ....GRETA LESKOVAR..................

was Cremated on the ....TWELFTH DAY OF MAY 1975.................., and that the

Cremains are in the sealed Container Numbered ....67101..........................

Garden State Crematory

4101 Kennedy Blvd., North Bergen, N. J. 07047
Phone: (201) 867-0219

Charles J. Morrin
General Manager

THIS BURIAL CERTIFICATE SHOULD ACCOMPANY THESE REMAINS TO THEIR DESTINATION

Certificate of Cremation. *Although there is no standard practice, cremated remains usually come with a receipt or certificate that identifies whose remains they are. This certificate is for the cremated remains of Greta Leskovar, my mother's stepmother. Most crematories are very careful and respectful about how they handle cremation. However, there are exceptions, such as crematories where groups of bodies were cremated at the same time and the collective cremated remains were randomly divided into different containers that the unsuspecting families thought contained only their loved one's remains. Then there was the case of a woman in Florida who started to scatter her husband's cremated remains and discovered dentures along with the bone fragments. Since her husband hadn't worn dentures, she knew something was wrong. Eventually she discovered that her husband's remains had been scattered from an airplane at sea, a fate that she and her husband had specifically ruled out. She sued the cremation society and was awarded half a million dollars.*

When I visited Ferncliff Mausoleum in Hartsdale, New York, a staff person pointed to the doors and gurney in this picture and said, "We use the gurney to transport the coffin to the crematory, which is right through those doors."

centuries later so did early Christians, who viewed cremation as a pagan practice of the Greco-Roman cultures. As Christians multiplied, so did the practice of inhumation, and by C.E. 400 in Europe it had completely replaced cremation, except during times of plagues and wars when dead bodies piled up. Eventually, however, in the late 1800s cremation was revived because rapidly growing populations had resulted in overcrowded cemeteries that were creating terrible odors and hazardous health conditions.

While cremation went in and out of favor in Europe, it has been practiced without interruption in other countries, such as Japan and India, where most corpses are cremated. In the United States cremation didn't take hold until the mid-1900s. Since then the number of cremations has steadily increased, and some experts predict that in the year 2010 close to 40 percent of all corpses in the United States will be cremated.

Major religious groups have different attitudes toward cremation. For Hindus and Buddhists it is a required part of their religious practice. Traditional Muslims and Orthodox Jews prohibit it. Conservative Jews generally do too. Reform Jews and many Protestant religions, including Methodists, Presbyterians, Episcopalians, and Jehovah's Witnesses, approve of cremation. The Roman Catholic Church has traditionally disapproved of cremation. "We have always looked at the body as the temple of the Holy Spirit," explained Bishop Frank Rodimer in a newspaper article, "Bishops May Ask Vatican to Permit Ashes at Mass." In 1968, perhaps in light of the fact that growing numbers of Catholics were being cremated, the Vatican allowed Catholics to be cremated after the funeral with a body and casket. However, that may soon change because nearly two hundred bishops in the United States recently asked permission from the Vatican to allow ashes to be present at a funeral mass.

Throughout history people developed different cremation rituals. Typically the corpse was placed on a pyre, or pile of combustible material, which was set on fire. Before burning a corpse

some prehistoric people covered it with red ocher. Ancient Babylonians wrapped the corpse in combustible material, put it in a clay coffin, and built the pyre around it. Ancient Romans had various traditions, including putting the uncoffined corpse on a pile of pine logs that had sweet-smelling gums stuffed between the logs. On some occasions, gladiators fought while it burned. The bone fragments were collected, washed with milk, and placed in a perfumed cinerary urn, or an urn intended to hold cremated remains. In Indonesia the Ma'anyan had a week-long festival to burn corpses in coffins that they had accumulated for several years. About a dozen at a time, the coffins were

This photograph, titled "Preparing Dead Bodies for Cremation," was taken in 1895 by William Henry Jackson along the bank of the Ganges River in the city of Banares (which before 1948 was spelled Benares). Hindus consider the Ganges the most sacred river in India and Banares a holy city.

stacked on a grating that was over a fire. The ash containing the bone fragments was collected and stored in large raised wooden containers in the graveyard.

Traditional Hindu cremation rituals required the widow to commit *suttee*, or burn herself to death on her dead husband's pyre. Although the practice was banned in 1929, suttee still occurs. In *The History of Doing,* her book about the women's rights movement and feminism in India, Radha Kumar reports that "there has been, on an average, something like one sati [suttee] a year in India." After the suttee of Roop Kanwar in 1987, a young woman whose husband died six months after they were married, a furor erupted and many people joined in an antisuttee movement to stop the practice.

Wives or unmarried women were sometimes added to the pyre as part of Viking cremation traditions. According to an eyewitness report by Al Massudi, a ninth-century Arab emissary: "They cremated their dead, and on the same funeral pile they laid the weapons of the dead, their beasts of burden, and their jewelry. When a man dies, his wife is cremated with him. But when the wife dies, her husband does not share her fate. When an unmarried man dies, they let him celebrate his marriage after death [this involved sacrificing a young woman]."

In C.E. 922 Ibn Fadlan, a diplomat from the caliph of Bagdad, witnessed the cremation of a Viking in his ship. After describing the lengthy process of dragging the ship onto the banks of the Volga River, dressing the corpse, and sacrificing a young woman, he writes, "And now the next of kin of the dead man stepped forward, picked up a piece of wood, set fire to it, and walked to the stern of the boat, the piece of wood in one hand, the other covering his buttock—for he was naked—until the wood under the boat was burning. Then others came also with pieces of wood burning at the tip, and threw them on the funeral pile. . . . And it did not take long for boat, wood and maiden, and the dead man to be reduced to ashes. On the spot where the boat that had been dragged out of the water had stood, they piled up a round mound in the middle of which they raised a pillar of beech-wood on which they inscribed the name of the dead man."

Just as people had different cremation traditions, so they had different reasons for cremation. The Franks, a Germanic tribe of people who lived in Europe from the third to the fifth century C.E., believed that if they cremated a dead person, it couldn't return to haunt living people. The Tlingit Indians practiced cremation to provide warmth for the dead person during the long and difficult journey to the spirit world. Some ancient Romans and Greeks believed that flame would set the soul free. In his book *Fire Burial Among Our Germanic Forefathers,* Karl Blind wrote: "The twirling flame which rose from the pyre towards Heaven did not fill them with the idea of final destruction. . . . They looked upon flame as a true conductor of the dead, as emancipator of the soul."

After battles the ancient Greeks built pyres and cremated the bodies of dead soldiers to prevent them from being desecrated; also, it was easier to bring bones back home to be honored and buried. During plagues many people have used cremation to handle the disposal of large numbers of bodies and to stop the

During times of plagues, corpses were frequently disposed of in unceremonious ways because of the fear of contamination and an overwhelming number of bodies. This print, titled View of the Manner of Burying the Dead Bodies at Holy-well Mount During the Dreadful Plague in 1665, *was engraved for* Chamberlain's History of London.

spread of disease. In addition cremated remains are neater to dispose of than corpses. They take up less room too. Since 1985 in China, the country with the world's largest population, people have been required to practice cremation in densely popu-

This photograph of a Native American burial scaffold was taken in 1912, probably in the southwestern United States, and titled "Tribute to the Dead." As I was ordering a print to use in this book, Maja Keech, a reference specialist in the Prints and Photograph Division at the Library of Congress, said, "I've always thought that's how I'd like to be treated after I'm dead."

lated areas, areas without much arable land, or where there is easy access to a crematorium.

So far in this book I've written about some common things that happen to corpses—decomposition, transplants, autopsies, embalming, and cremation. Uncommon things happen too. In his book *Psyche and Death*, Edgar Herzog writes that a number of people disposed of corpses by letting wild dogs or wolves eat them: "In Lhasa [Tibet] and other towns and temples special dogs are kept, and they destroy the dead bodies with astounding appetite. In many temples the corpse-eating dogs are regarded as holy, and a man acquires merit by allowing his dead body to be eaten by them." Some nomadic people of central Asia cut corpses into small pieces and left them as food for wild animals. In the tenth century, certain types of sinners that the Catholic Church refused to bury were left to rot after a chant was said over the body, *Sint cadavera eorum, in escam volatilibus coeli, et bestiis terra,* or, "Give over this erring body for food to the fowls of the air and beasts of the field."

In some times and places, people have left corpses in trees and on high platforms. In the United States, many Native American Plains tribes did this in order to speed up decomposition, therefore expediting the soul's journey to the spirit world. In New Zealand, the Maoris frequently placed dead bodies on the branches or hollow trunk of a tree as part of their burial ceremony known as *tangi,* meaning "to cry." The Parsi, a religious group who practice the ancient Persian religion Zoroastrianism, believe that earth, fire, and water are sacred and should never be contaminated by contact with decaying flesh. Since ancient times they have erected large towers on hills, known as Towers of Silence, where they left dead bodies to be eaten by vultures. Usually within an hour, the vultures had done their job, and an attendant placed the skeleton into a central shaft. In 1876 Professor Monier Williams witnessed the process and wrote, "Two bearers speedily unlocked the door, reverently conveyed the body . . . into the interior, and . . . laid it uncovered in one of the open stone receptacles nearest the central well. . . . Scarcely had they closed the door when a dozen vultures swooped down upon the body, and were rapidly followed by others. . . . [Then] we saw the satiated birds fly back and lazily settle down again upon the parapet. . . . The same bearers return, and with gloved hands and implements resembling tongs place the dry skeleton in the central well. There the bones find their last resting-place, and there the dust of whole generations of Parsi commingling is left undisturbed for centuries." Today about 120,000 Parsi live in New Delhi, India, where they continue their ancient practice. Parsi who live in other places that either prohibit exposing dead bodies or don't have Towers of Silence practice cremation.

Corpses have also been boiled, eaten, left on mountains, and lost at sea. "A corpse interred in water becomes an ugly, smelly mess," writes Kenneth Iserson. "Bodies exposed to water decompose approximately four times faster than in earth, and if the water is warm or polluted, the corruption occurs much faster." And yes, fish, crabs, and small marine animals that are around will feed on corpses. Bodies found floating in the cold water of San Francisco Bay routinely have "shrimps at the orifices," says Dr. Joseph Carr. Corpses also have been divided up and disposed of in pieces. It was fashionable in the Middle Ages to bury the heart in containers made of different materials, including gold, ivory, and earthenware. In the nineteenth century the hearts of the poet John Keats, who died in Italy, and the explorer David Livingstone, who died in Africa, were removed and sent back to England for burial.

Although to date the challenge of disposing of corpses has been met with a variety of solutions, nowadays some people have decided not to dispose of corpses at all but to preserve them for future revival. By using cryonics, the practice of freezing dead bodies at extremely low temperatures, the bodies of people who have died from a particular disease are preserved so that they can be revived if a cure is discovered. Of course no one knows whether future technology will ever make it possible to revive any of these people even if cures are found. According to

F.M. Brown Inscription on a Boulder in the Grand Canyon. *In 1986 I took a white-water raft trip down the Colorado River through the Grand Canyon in Arizona. One night after setting up camp on a narrow, sandy beach, I hiked upstream, scrambled over boulders, and discovered an inscription marking the death of F. M. Brown scratched into a ledge just above the river. Brown, president of the Denver, Colorado Canyon & Pacific Railroad Company, wanted to build a railroad through the Grand Canyon. During an expedition to survey a route, however, Brown drowned, and his body was never recovered. Brown's friend Peter Hansborough carved the inscription on the boulder, which reads: "F.M. Brown Pres. D.C.C. & P.R.R. Co. was drowned July 10, 1889, opposite this point." Five days later Hansborough himself drowned at 25 Mile Rapid.*

an article, "The Iceman Goeth," in the *Los Angeles Times*, critics like Arthur Rowe, past president of the Society for Cryobiology, which studies organisms at low temperatures, compares it to "trying to make hamburger back into a cow." Advocates, however, say that they have nothing to lose because the frozen people are dead anyway. As of 1994, Alcor Life Extension Foundation, the world's leading cryonics company, had twenty-seven frozen "patients" and some pets, who are suspended in Dacron sleeping bags in stainless steel tanks filled with liquid nitrogen.

Regardless of what happens to corpses—from inhumation and cremation to cryonic suspension—most of them get put into things. And people have found a variety of ways to contain corpses and cremated remains.

·five·

How to Contain the Remains: Urns, Coffins, Crypts, and Mausoleums

Willi's cremated remains were in a bronze, rectangular-shaped urn. "Since he was an average-size man, an urn with a capacity of two hundred cubic inches would be big enough," the funeral director told me. "What if he had been a professional basketball player?" I asked. "Then I would have sold you the urn with a capacity of three hundred cubic inches," he said.

Throughout history urns have been made from a myriad of materials, including terra-cotta, stone, crystalline rock, alabaster, bronze, silver, gold, and ceramic. They have been tall, short, round, square, rectangular, with and without necks, with straight or curved sides, and decorated in a variety of ways. Some urns have a unique look, such as the house-shaped urns that the ancient Romans used. Today in the United States, people can buy a keepsake urn, or a small urn that holds a small portion of the cremated remains, in case families want to divide up the cremated remains for burial in different places. "For example, I want some of my cremated remains to be in the Bahamas," explained Jack Springer, executive director of the Cremation Association. "And the rest can be divided among my four grown

Containing cremated remains can be expensive. The prices for the urns in this modern display case range from $3,500 for the one in the middle of the third row from the bottom to $225 for the third one from the right in the second row from the bottom.

children, who live in different parts of the country." Keepsake urns come in a variety of shapes, including leaping dolphins and angels.

Different things have been done with urns. The Assyrians buried urns in graves. The Etruscans put cremated remains in large jars that were placed on supports. The Zapotecs placed urns in special hills called *mogotes*. The ancient Romans placed urns in an immense underground structure with rows of niches called a columbarium, a word that is derived from the Latin word *columba*, meaning dove, because doves make their nests in a dovecote, or nesting area that is made up of many niches. After the urns were cemented to the bottom of the niche, the niche was sealed, except for a small opening that was left so that mourners could pour in offerings of milk and wine. In modern Buddhist countries, urns are kept on home altars. In the United States, urns are typically buried in graves or placed in aboveground columbaria. It is also common to scatter the cremated remains in gardens, bodies of water, and the wilderness. Jay Knudsen, owner of Canuck's Sportsman's Memorials in Des Moines, Iowa, has put cremated remains of hunters in shotgun shells so that they could be shot where the hunter loved to hunt. He has also put them into other sports equipment, including fishing lures, the shafts of golf clubs, and

In keeping with the desert surroundings, a sculpture of a Gambrel's quail decorates a contemporary columbarium in Twentynine Palms, California.

basketballs. In 1996 a new company, Celestis, announced its plans to launch cremated remains into orbit in space. On April 21, 1997, a rocket was launched into outer space with the cremated remains of twenty-four people, including Gene Roddenberry, who created the *Star Trek* television series. People who want to keep someone's cremated remains close by can have them put into jewelry and objects such as glass sculptures.

As for uncremated human remains, sometimes they were contained and sometimes they weren't. In his book *Funeral Customs*, Bertram Puckle writes: "In early days in England the bodies of the poor were committed to the grave practically naked, or at best wrapped in a shroud of linen." In other times and places, corpses that were to be buried were put in a variety of things—jars; baskets woven of plaited twigs; animal skins; cerecloth, or cloth treated with melted wax or gummy material; shrouds, or a white garment that was generally made of linen or wool and resembled a long-sleeved nightgown; and winding sheets, or a sheet with the ends tied or sewn shut to make a sack. Some knights were put in a full set of armor and then buried. In France in the eighteenth century, the bark of a chestnut tree, a tree that was highly valued for the beauty of its wood and its edible chestnut, was wrapped around the bodies of dead children until a law was passed against it because too many trees were being ruined. In the Tigre province of Ethiopia, a corpse was typically first wrapped in a fresh sheet of calico or muslin, or satin if the person was a noble. Then it was placed in an outer wrapper that was made from palm leaves.

Removing the Shell of the Outer-Most Coffin of Tutankhamen. In ancient Egypt a mummy was typically contained in a series of different-size coffins, or mummy cases. The mummy cases were elaborately decorated with paintings and spells that the Egyptians believed would protect the body and help its spirit on the arduous journey through the afterlife. The archaeologists who excavated the pharaoh Tutankhamen's tomb removed two mummy cases before they discovered his mummy inside the third, or inner, case, which was made of solid gold. This picture was taken in 1926 and titled "Removing the Shell of the Outer-most Coffin of Tut-Ankh-Amen." The original caption read: "The necessary tackle to lower the shell of the first or outermost coffin from the second coffin of Tut-Ankh-Amen. The second coffin fitted so closely in the first coffin that it could not be lifted out in the ordinary way, the shell of the first coffin had thus to be lowered from it."

V 17150 Greek Sarcophagus of Roman Period, Nat. Museum, Athens, Greece.

Ancient Egyptians put dead people in mummy cases that evolved from plain rectangular wooden coffins to beautifully decorated mummy cases that were made in the shape of the human body. Sometimes a series of different-size mummy cases were placed inside each other, one after another. The Egyptians also used a sarcophagus, or a coffin made from stone. The first stone coffins were made from a particular type of stone that supposedly had the power to eat flesh; therefore they were called sarcophagi, or "flesh eating." In addition to wood and stone, coffins have been made of a wide variety of materials, including bricks covered with tiles, terra-cotta, hollowed-out logs, lead, glass, and metal. Coffins have been plain; richly carved; covered with jewels, silver, and gold; and lined with everything from tin to taffeta. Straw was generally used to line slaves' coffins in the United States, although sometimes cambric and lace were used. Coffins have been made with four

Stereo view card of an ancient Greek sarcophagus displayed in the National Museum in Athens, Greece. Between 1850 and 1930, stereo view cards that were inserted into a viewer called a stereograph were popular in the United States. Two nearly identical photographs were pasted on the cards. When viewed through the stereograph, the two photographs appeared as one three-dimensional image.

sides, six sides, and eight sides; with rounded and squared corners; and with one- or two-part tops. At one time in Scotland, some coffins had a removable side. Other coffins, known as slip coffins, had a hinged bottom. Both of these types of coffins were used to carry the corpse to the grave, where it was dropped out of the bottom or side, thus making the coffin reusable. In the United States today, coffins are available for people to rent for the funeral. After the service the corpse is transferred to an inexpensive casket that has been purchased for the burial or cremation.

People used coffins for a variety of reasons. For some people it was a way to protect the corpse. Other people viewed coffins as a way to confine dead spirits. Other people thought that coffins were a way to honor a dead person. In modern-day Ghana, the Ga believe that the funeral must be properly done or the dead person's spirit will suffer. So they spare no expense for the type of coffin they provide. For the funeral of a man who had spent his life leading sardine-fishing expeditions, his family hired Paa Joe, a skilled craftsperson, to make a coffin shaped like a sardine.

In the United States, the first colonists were buried without coffins. But by the 1700s, people were hiring carpenters and cabinetmakers to make coffins. Typically the corpse was brought to the carpenter's shop and measured. If that wasn't possible, someone would cut a stick the same length as the dead person and take the stick to the carpenter. David Evans, an eighteenth-century cabinetmaker in Philadelphia, kept a journal that included these entries:

1788: Nov. 26 This morning a fire broke out next door to the Bunch of Grapes, in Third St. near Arch— consumed the house in which were eight persons, five of whom got out, and three, the widow Preston and her two sons, were burned before assistance could be given. Making a Coffin for the three remains found in ruins.

1792: Nov. 20 Mr. Randolph, Attorney General U.S., making a Coffin for his black servant.

1793: Mar. 7 Daniel Rundle, making a Coffin for his wife Ann Rundle, covered with Black Cloth, lined with White Flannel, Inscription Plate, Flowerpots and Cherubs, Handles, and full laced.

Sept. 11 Estate of my brother Richard Gardner, a Walnut Coffin. He died of Yellow Fever. Was a Clerk in the Bank of Pennsylvania and an admirable accountant. Buried in Friends' Ground.

During the nineteenth century, coffin making became a full-time business. Coffin shops were established, and patents were taken out for all kinds of coffins, including a coffin that was adjustable in size. In the second half of the nineteenth century, the term *casket* came into regular use. Although *casket* and *coffin* are frequently used interchangeably, the terms do mean different things: a coffin is the traditional wedge-shaped, simple container for a corpse, and a casket, which originally meant a jewel box, is a rectangular-shaped container that typically is fancier than a coffin. Today Americans can buy a wide variety

Amana Coffin. The Amana Colony in Iowa was established in 1855 by descendants of a religious movement that started in Germany. Today modern business practices govern the economic life of the community while the Amana Church remains the religious force. "Whether you're a millionaire or only have two dollars, you get buried alike here," Midge Albert told me during my visit to Amana. I photographed this display of an Amana coffin in the store that sells Amana furniture. The photographs on the wall are of an Amana cemetery and a woman staining a coffin. Excerpts from the captions on the wall are: "In the cemetery of Amana . . . the deceased are buried in rows in order of their death. Headstones are placed seven feet apart, all facing east. . . . Each lists only the name and death date of the deceased. . . . Funeral services were brief and simple. Flowers and open demonstrations of emotions were discouraged, and the funeral processions were quiet and austere. . . . The casket was made of stained pine, and constructed in a simple way, with no ornamentation. The long boards were joined with wooden pegs. The lids were hinged with wooden pins, and there were wooden handles on each side. When the casket was completed, it was lined with white muslin, and a pillow stuffed with shavings from the wood of the casket was placed inside. The casket would sit for a short time in an almost empty room, with a clock with the hands stopped at the time of death."

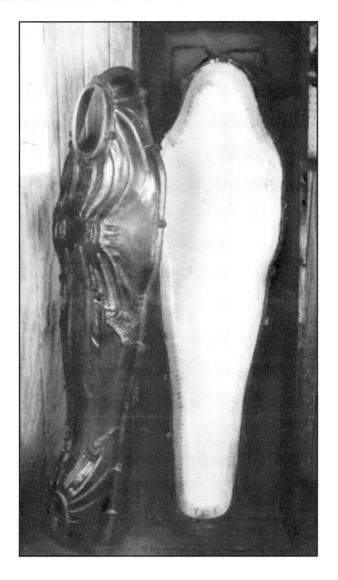

Patented in 1848 as the Fiske Metallic Burial Case, this coffin was shaped as a human body with the arms crossed across the chest. The face was visible through a glass window. It was endorsed in an advertisement that appeared in the New York Tribune *in April 1850 that included a testimony from several leading statesmen, including Henry Clay and Daniel Webster, who wrote: "Gentlemen: We witnessed the utility of our ornamental Patent Metallic Burial Case used to convey the remains of the late Hon. John C. Calhoun to the Congressional Cemetery. It impressed us with the belief that it is the best article known to us for transporting the dead to their final resting place."*

of caskets made of various metals or woods and lined with various materials, including satin. Custom-made caskets are available for extra-tall and extra-wide people or for people who want a one-of-a-kind casket, like the ones that Dr. and Mrs. Hiller designed for themselves in the late 1880s.

James MacGregor and four assistants spent about seven years, at forty dollars a week, making the caskets that the Hillers had designed. Four-inch-thick mahogany was used, and the outside was carved with ivy vines, a skull, angels, cupids, bats flying about the heads of serpents, and a big owl with a mouse in its claws. Eight brass lion's paws were placed inside to support a steel hammock. Gold and silver plates with portraits of the Hillers and their twenty-three children, all of whom had died in infancy, including seven sets of twins, were mounted to the top of each casket.

Before his casket was finished, Dr. Hiller died, but his body was kept in a vault until his casket was ready. About a year later, the casket was completed and Hiller was buried in Wildwood Cemetery in Wilmington, Massachusetts, after a lavish funeral. In another three and a half years, Mrs. Hiller's casket was finished. Thoroughly pleased with it, she set it up in her parlor and showed it to her friends, frequently climbing in to demonstrate how she would look. Finally she had a wax model of herself

If a grave could not be dug due to severe weather conditions, the coffin was kept in this "receiving tomb." Today it is not used because funeral homes have storage areas. Oak Hill Cemetery, Nyack, New York.

made and placed in the casket. The robes for the model cost twenty thousand dollars and had five thousand daisies embroidered on the lace. Eventually Mrs. Hiller's money ran low, so she had eight truck horses haul the casket with the wax model to Boston, where she put it on display in Horticultural Hall and charged admission. When Mrs. Hiller died, four black horses draped in black netting pulled the casket on its bier to the grave beside her husband.

While the Hillers' caskets were interred, or put into the ground, there is a long tradition of human remains being entombed or placed above the ground in a building called a mausoleum, after King Mausolus of Caria, who had an elaborate building constructed as a tomb in about 352 B.C.E. Located in Halicarnassus, the building was considered one of the Seven Wonders of the World. It was destroyed in the thirteenth or fourteenth century, probably by an earthquake. Some parts sur-

Since New Orleans, Louisiana, lies below sea level, the ground is watery and all interments are aboveground. People who could not afford to build a tomb were buried in these half-oval-shaped cells. "They bake their dead in ovens," one visitor wrote home.

Top right: *Renowned architects and builders were frequently involved in building the first mausoleums in the United States, including the Cathedral of Memories in Hartsdale, New York, which is considered a classic. The remains of more than eight thousand people are contained in niches and crypts.* Left: *These urns are placed in niches with a choice of a marble cover or glass cover (shown). The person's name and dates of birth and death were engraved on the urn and on a bronze plate under the glass cover or carved directly on the marble cover.* Bottom right: *Most of the crypts at Hartsdale are six rows high and at least six rows wide. In this picture about halfway between the vases of flowers is one row of crypts where the coffin must be slid in headfirst. The rest of the crypts are wide enough so that the coffin can be slid in sideways. Judy Garland is buried in the bottom crypt behind the first vase of flowers, which are regularly provided by her fan club. Niches start at $950. A crypt for one person is $6,900. A grave in the ground for two bodies—one buried on top of the other—is $2,200. The only markers allowed outside are flat bronze plaques. Malcolm X is buried there under a plaque that also has his Muslim name: El Hajj-Malik El Shabazz.*

vived and are now in the British Museum. Other mausoleums were built in other times and places. The ancient Romans built ones big enough to hold seven hundred bodies. In India, after the Empress Mumtaz Mahal requested that her husband build her the most magnificent mausoleum that the world had seen, he had the Taj Mahal built. In Campo Santo, the twelfth-century cemetery in Pisa, Italy, people built lavish mausoleums for themselves and their families. A huge mausoleum was built in Tiananmen Square in Beijing, China, to display in a glass casket the embalmed body of Mao Zedong, the founder of the People's Republic of China, who died in 1976. When I was in Beijing in 1980, I joined a very slow-moving, long line of people who were waiting to view Mao's body. No one was allowed to linger as we passed close by the open casket. My impression was of a waxy appearance and benign expression on Mao's face. As of 1997, lines of people still wait to view Mao's body. According to a recent guidebook to China, tourists are advised, "Dignified dress and behavior is expected. Photography is not permitted."

Although mausoleums were typically built by and for rich people, new types of mausoleums appeared in the late 1800s, especially in the United States. Typically built in cemeteries and known as community mausoleums, these were places where people without huge sums of money could be entombed in a compartment called a crypt, a new use of a word that originally referred to an underground room or vault that was usually under a church. The word *crypt* comes from the Greek word *kryptein*, meaning to hide. Throughout history religious

In this small section of Rock Creek Cemetery in Washington, D.C., there is a mausoleum (the chapel-like structure behind the tree on the left), four crypts in the hill (four doors along the road), a bronze sarcophagus (in between the two trees in the foreground), and an assortment of gravestones that mark in-ground graves.

martyrs and saints were often buried in crypts, and today people visit famous crypts, including the one of Saint Helena in Jerusalem.

Today mausoleums with niches for urns and crypts for caskets are being promoted and advertised. Recently I received an unsolicited advertisement urging me to "*act now, and get 40 percent off,*" and buy a place in their new mausoleum because it was an "*aboveground burial—the clean burial. Isn't that the way you and your family want to be remembered? Does the thought of belowground burial disturb you? There is an alternative, you know. Aboveground burial, the clean burial.*" Because I love to garden, I'm quite fond of dirt, so the ad didn't appeal to me. However, I know other people will respond. "My wife recently bought two spots in one of those places, even though I had already bought a cemetery plot for two graves," Peter Amicucci told me. "I don't want to be buried in a drawer, but she doesn't

This crypt was built for the sarcophagus of John Paul Jones. A naval hero of the Revolutionary War, John Paul Jones uttered the words, "I have not yet begun to fight," in reply to a British officer's demand to surrender. Jones died in Paris, France, and was buried there. More than a hundred years later General Horace Porter decided to bring Jones's body back to America. It took Porter years to find the grave. When Porter finally had Jones's body disinterred, he was amazed to discover that it was in excellent condition, most likely because Jones's limbs had been wrapped in tinfoil and his coffin was made of lead.

like the idea of dirt and worms. I keep telling her that you won't know the difference once you're dead."

Regardless of how cremated remains or corpses are contained or whether they end up aboveground or underground, most of them end up in cemeteries; places that I find fascinating.

· s i x ·

Where Corpses End Up:
Cemeteries and Other Burial Sites

I've always loved cemeteries—they're brimming with art, architecture, history, horticulture, and stories, lots of stories. Other people love cemeteries too. "I really love cemeteries!" Alison Noble, a sixth grader, wrote me. "I was born in England and often go back to visit. On my most recent visit, I went with my friends and family to about five or six different cemeteries. We tried to find the earliest date on the gravestones. At one cemetery I saw a headstone with the figure of a baby. I read the headstone, and everyone in the family had died. I felt so bad for these people that I picked some flowers and stuck them in the baby's arms."

Lindsay Koehler is exuberant about cemeteries. "I love cemeteries! They are very peaceful and relaxing. My husband and I had one of our first dates in a cemetery!" Doug Marion echoed Lindsay's words. "Cemeteries are wonderful, quiet, peaceful places," he said during our conversation about the six summers he spent working at a cemetery. "The summer before I went to college, I just went to the cemetery and asked, 'Are you hiring?'" They were and Doug started out cutting grass, but

before long he was doing different jobs. He cleaned up dead flowers and set up chairs for funerals. If the gravediggers were digging a new grave beside an old grave, he helped them build a wooden frame so that the dirt from the side of the old grave wouldn't cave into the new grave. Since the coffin would fill up part of the hole, there was the excess dirt that Doug had to haul away. When there was a funeral, he met the hearse and helped take out the coffin. "Once we opened the back door and no body! It turned out that the driver had taken the wrong hearse, and everyone had to wait about an hour until the right hearse showed up. The driver was really upset, the mourners were understanding, and my coworkers and I thought that it was very funny, although we acted dignified," Doug remembered.

Long before the appearance of cemeteries as we know them today, people have been burying dead bodies or cremated remains in the ground. Throughout history, in fact, most dead bodies have been buried in the ground, or inhumed. Burial sites have been discovered with skeletons of Neanderthals, a prehistoric people who lived during Paleolithic times, between 35,000 and 135,000 years ago. Because the skeletons were found carefully arranged in a grave, scientists concluded that they were intentionally buried, not just left where they died. As for people who lived during Neolithic times, which started with the development of farming about nine thousand years ago, there is no doubt that they left behind burial sites. The Natufians, who lived in the area of present-day Palestine, created a cemetery in a rock shelter that contains the graves of eighty-seven people. The people who lived in Jericho, one of the earliest Neolithic

Depending on the type of ground, digging a grave with hand tools takes between three and eight hours. Today most graves are dug in twenty minutes by a person operating a machine called a backhoe. These two men had to dig this grave with a shovel and pickax because there wasn't enough room to maneuver a backhoe.

villages, buried dead people under the floors of their houses. The skeletons—without their skulls—of forty people were found in one house. The skulls, it appears, were removed and displayed as a way to honor the dead person. With the exception of one skull, none of them had a lower jaw, which was left attached to the skeleton. The skulls were covered with plaster that was carefully modeled so that each skull had an individual look, as if someone had attempted to reproduce the appearance

After a grave is dug, a liner or vault is typically placed inside it. The contraption over the top is a removable lowering device that cemetery workers use to lower the casket into the grave. An AstroTurf–type material is placed over the dirt around the lowering device.

of the dead person. One skull had a painted-on mustache. Every skull had seashells in the eye sockets.

Neolithic cemeteries have been discovered around the world. Many of them are barrows, or different shapes and sizes of mounds of earth with bodies buried in or under them. Neolithic bodies have also been discovered in shafts, pits, and tombs lined with sun-baked mud bricks. The residents of Eridu, one of the earliest Neolithic cities in the area of present-day Iran, created a cemetery with at least one thousand graves. Bodies were placed in boxes that were made from mud bricks. Some families used the same box by reopening it when the need arose and inserting another body. In 1980 I visited the site of 250 Neolithic graves in China near the present-day village of Ban Po, six miles east of Xian. All the skeletons were buried with their heads pointing toward the west. The bodies of small children were buried in large pottery vessels. Two men were buried together in one grave, four girls were buried together in one grave, and all the rest of the graves contained one person.

Marlise Johnson, who grew up on the island of Amrum, remembers when archaeologists discovered Neolithic graves in the sand dunes and marshes. The graves were in mounds of earth and topped with circles of large stones. "My friends and I were all ten years old, and we knew that we could get in trouble for digging," she said. "But when we heard that the archaeologists had

This postcard pictures the stones that marked the Neolithic cemetery on Amrum.

discovered amber, we went nuts anyhow and dug up half the island before we quit without finding anything."

Shortly before 3000 B.C.E., people who lived in the Tigris-Euphrates Valley, in present-day Iraq, invented writing, and that is considered the end of the Neolithic period. Now people could write history and the period that has been labeled prehistory was over. People had come a long way from barely surviving as Paleolithic hunters and gatherers. They had learned how to grow crops, domesticate plants, and raise animals. Populations were soaring, civilizations were rising, and even more cemeteries were needed. As they had in the past, people met this need in a variety of ways.

In the Nile Valley, the ancient Egyptians built thousands of cemeteries. Some contained graves that were mostly oval-shaped and located outside the settlement. Others were filled with mastabas, or flat-topped, aboveground tombs with steeply sloping sides. Chambers, shafts, and hidden burial rooms were built in the mastabas and under the ground. Because streets ran between the rows of mastabas, the area became known as a

The first known pyramid in Egypt. It is called the Step Pyramid of Djoser, after the king, and is located at the site of the ancient city of Saqqara.

necropolis, or "city of the dead." The first pyramid, the burial sites for royalty, was built in about 2650 B.C.E. when Imhotep, a physician, architect, and statesman, conceived of stacking mastabas atop one another. Elaborate tombs were built as burial sites in other parts of Africa, including in the ancient kingdom of Ghana in western Sudan. In the kingdom of Aksum in the Ethiopian highlands, granite stelae, or stone pillars with carvings or inscriptions, were erected over the graves of royalty. The largest one still standing today is seventy-one feet high. In the Rift Valley of Kenya, burial sites were covered with cairns, or heaps of stones, some of which had stone-lined shafts at the center and were up to fifty feet across.

On another continent, North America, in about 1000 B.C.E. the Adena and Hopewell people, who lived north of the Ohio

More than a thousand years ago people who are now known as Mound Builders situated this burial mound at the confluence of the Mississippi and Ohio Rivers in the present-day town of Wickliffe, Kentucky. Archaeologists began excavations in 1932 and created exhibits for people to view. This picture is one of a series of postcards that were made of the area. Grave goods are visible next to some of the skeletons.

General View of the Adult Burial Tomb, Ancient Buried City
Wickliffe, Kentucky

Valley and west of the Mississippi River in the present-day United States, began building dirt burial mounds. At first a small mound of dirt was placed over bodies that were buried in a shallow bark-lined grave or cremated in fire-reddened clay basins. In time other bodies were buried on top of the first mound and then covered with dirt so that the mound got higher, some up to seventy-one feet. For 1,700 years people built burial mounds throughout the United States, including in what are now known as the states of Oklahoma, West Virginia, and Georgia. In New Hampshire, near Lake Ossipee, a Native American tribe built a mound that was originally about twenty-five feet high, seventy-five feet long, and fifty feet wide. During excavations a number of circles of skeletons were found. In each circle the skeletons were facing outward, apparently in sitting positions around the common center. It was estimated that the mound contained no fewer than eight thousand bodies.

About C.E. 200 the early Christians, who lived in Rome, the capital of the Roman Empire, used elaborate subterranean cemeteries of connecting corridors and rooms, known as catacombs, in the soft volcanic rock that surrounded the city. Modern experts estimate that six million Christians were buried in the catacombs around Rome and if the corridors were put end to end, they would stretch six hundred miles. Catacombs were also built in other cities in Italy, North Africa, and France. The actual graves were cut into the walls, and the walls were frequently painted with religious scenes and portraits of religious leaders. In order to reduce odors the bodies were usually covered in plaster and sealed in the tombs, and perfumes were constantly burned. When the first level of catacomb was filled, the second level was built under it. Some catacombs went down six levels. During the time when Christians were persecuted, they took refuge in the catacombs because burial grounds were considered sacred under a Roman law that read: "Every person makes the place that belongs to him a religious place by the carrying of his dead into it."

In the late C.E. 300s, when Christianity became the official religion of the Roman Empire, Christians changed their burial sites to traditional tombs and graves, and the catacombs were eventually forgotten. In 1578, however, they were rediscovered when a person digging in a Roman vineyard accidentally broke through into a tunnel and saw a narrow passage lined on each side with tomb niches. Since then the catacombs have been very popular. Christians make pilgrimages to pray and hold religious services. Tourists come to sightsee. In his book *A Traveler in Rome*, H. V. Morton describes his visit to the Catacomb of St. Domitilla in Rome: "Grasping a taper, I followed an English group [of tourists] which descended on the heels of a French group; and no sooner had we left the daylight behind than the chill of the catacombs came up and gripped us like a bony hand. Even the humorist of the party, who had been lively enough at the ticket office, fell silent after a half-hearted attempt at facetiousness and we walked in single file into a darkness lit only by the flickering of our tapers. Like bunks in a ship the burial niches rose one above the other in the rough walls. . . . One's first feeling of dismay at finding oneself in this dusty maze of death is soon replaced by an affectionate fellow feeling for those who had lived so long before us."

Throughout history most people thought about where they created burial sites. "Any Malagasy who has to choose a tomb-site [which should be south-east or south-west of the village] is faced with a major decision because so many crucial *fady* (taboos) are involved," Dervla Murphy writes in her book about Madagascar. "A wrongly placed tomb may lead to early deaths in the family so the *ombiasa* (loosely translated as witch-doctor) has to advise on the exactly right spot. The tomb door must face west but not due west, to avoid giving it the same *vintana* (destiny) as the family home; because the dead have a stronger *vintana* than the living, a shared alignment would put them in a dangerously powerful position. No tomb must be built at the end of a valley, or where it can be seen from a village, and the building of it must take more than one year." In Korea a burial site had to be out of sight of the "baleful spirits" in order to protect the dead person. In China the choice of a site was based on an ancient way of divining the magical forces that flow through the landscape, known as geomancy, or *feng-shui*, which literally means "wind-water." A geomancer, or *feng-shui* master, follows general principles of *feng-shui*. In her book *The Imperial Ming Tombs*, Ann Paludan writes: "The first principle is that the place must be protected from the evil spirits which come from the dominant—usually the north—wind. The second is that water should not run through the site . . . but should, if possible, run in front of it (because if the course of the stream is altered the spirit will take offense). The third is that it is desirable to have a view of mountains with auspicious shapes. These mountains should be continuous, that is, it should not be possible to see clefts or passage through them. In other words, the

These signs are in a cemetery in New Orleans, Louisiana, where all interments are aboveground because the city lies below sea level.

ideal site is very much what people would look for today—a sheltered place, facing in a southerly direction, dry but with a stream nearby and a good view."

Worried about the health hazards of decaying corpses, the ancient Jews and Romans created burial sites outside the city walls. Germanic tribes—the Franks and Saxons—put their cemeteries far away from where people lived too, but for a very different reason—they feared that dead people might harm living people. Just as many people paid close attention to the location of the grave, they also paid attention to how the corpse was positioned in the grave. Slaves in the United States typically

A single or double-depth grave (buried one on top of the other) in Brookside Cemetery, Englewood, New Jersey, ranges from $900 to $1,250, plus $750 for Perpetual Care, which "provides for seeding and fertilizing and maintenance of the plot." A cremation plot and an infant grave up to three feet is $375. After paying the full amount, the person receives a deed to the plot. Although people typically buy a plot when there is a "need," because a relative has died, some people select their burial site, plan their funerals, and pay for everything "preneed," or before they die. Other people join burial societies, also known as memorial or funeral societies. The basic idea is that members pay a regular fee and the society takes care of the funeral arrangements, including providing mourners. Burial societies have existed since ancient times. Today burial societies are organized by a variety of groups, including religious organizations and labor unions to provide lower-than-usual-cost funerals for their members.

dug their graves from east to west and buried the body with its head to the west and feet to the east. "The dead should not have to turn around when Gabriel blows his trumpet [on Resurrection Day] in the eastern sunrise," writes Eugene Genovese in his book *Roll, Jordan, Roll.* Muslims are buried with their face turned toward Mecca, the most holy city in Islam.

As Christianity spread, particularly throughout Europe, Christians created cemeteries under the floors of their churches and cathedrals, sacred places that they thought would ensure their future in heaven. A section of the tile or stone church floor would be opened and a body buried in the earth underneath it. Not mummified bodies or decomposed-down-to-the-bones bod-

The Old Jewish Cemetery in Prague, the Czech Republic, is called Beth Chaim *in Hebrew, meaning "House of Life." As early as the tenth century, when Jews probably first settled in Prague, laws were passed that restricted many aspects of their lives, including how much space they could use for cemeteries. Bodies were buried in this cemetery from the fifteenth century until 1787, one on top of another and as many as eleven layers deep. The rakish angles of some of the grave-stones were caused by over-crowding and the weather.*

ies, just decaying bodies, which were usually wrapped in cere-cloth and placed in a coffin. Over and over this was done, and in time the whole floor got higher, sometimes to the point of meeting the lower windows of the church. Then bodies were buried in the churchyard. To cope with overcrowding, church officials started surreptitiously removing bones and partly decayed remains and piling them in *ossuaries*, or storehouses for bones.

The situation became overwhelming as plagues swept through Europe and millions of people died. Ossuaries were built just to accommodate the bones of plague victims. In 1996 my son Jonathan and his partner, Katrin de Haën, toured an ossuary in the Czech Republic near Kutná Hora that had been built to hold the bones of thirty thousand people who died in the plague of 1318. The Schwarzenberg family acquired the ossuary in 1783, and in 1870 they commissioned František Rinta to arrange the bones in a decorative manner. Using nothing but bones, Rinta built religious symbols, the Schwarzenberg family crest, and a huge chandelier that is strung with skulls and every other bone in the human body. "Kutná Horrid!" was Katrin's reaction. Jonathan agreed. "Seeing the bones arranged like they were toys was gross," they said.

By the 1700s the cemetery situation in Europe was a disaster. A visitor to France in 1775 described the cemeteries in Paris: "There are several burial pits in Paris, of a prodigious size and depth, in which the dead bodies are laid, side by side, without any earth being put over them till the ground tier is full; then, and not till then, a small layer of earth covers them, and another layer of dead comes on, till by layer upon layer, and dead upon dead, the hole is filled with a mass of human corruption enough to breed a plague." Stories about the dangers of decaying bodies were repeated over and over. According to one story, two hundred parishioners, forty children, and two church officials died after an "evil exhalation" arose from a tomb that had been dug on the same day beneath the church floor. Another story was told about a cellar wall that collapsed under the weight of neighboring tombs. Witnesses swore to the fact that the smell asphyxiated the owner of the cellar.

Ordinary citizens and reformers demanded changes, and finally the great cemetery cleanup in Europe began. In Paris six million bodies were removed from graveyards and buried in quarries outside the city limits, an undertaking that took eighteen months. Working at night by the light of torches, workers filled up carts with bones and remains. As they pulled the carts through the streets, priests walked alongside saying prayers while startled passersby retrieved bones that fell off. After much dis-

Today people can take tours of the ossuary near Kutná Hora in the Czech Republic and see a chandelier that contains every single bone in the human body as well as the Schwarzenburg family crest.

cussion about what were safe burial practices, new regulations were passed. In 1804 Père Lachaise, a new cemetery named after Jesuit friar François d'Aix de la Chaize, was opened. Because it was designed as both a burial place for dead people and a rural retreat for city dwellers, Père Lachaise is called the world's first

modern cemetery. To entice customers the remains of famous French citizens—among them the medieval lovers Abelard and Héloïse and the dramatist Molière—were exhumed and buried in Père Lachaise.

Within ten years it was clear that celebrated corpses and a

Frédéric Chopin's grave in Père Lachaise, with his name inscribed as A. Fred. Chopin.

beautiful setting were irresistible. Père Lachaise had become a prestigious burial site and was famous for its monuments. Guidebooks were published for the tourists who flocked to sightsee and city dwellers who came for outings. It is still a popular place. Some people are just curious. Other people have a mission like the high school junior I met who told me about her trip to Père Lachaise to find Jim Morrison's grave. "I had been thinking about laying a red rose on his grave for a long time, and I was so happy when I finally did it," she said. Frances Treanor went looking for

Frédéric Chopin's grave. "My mother, Alice, was an accomplished piano player and she played Chopin's waltzes beautifully. As I stood at his grave, I could hear my mother playing in my head. A friend who was with me couldn't recall any music by Chopin. So I thought about whistling a waltz, but then I remembered that I was in a cemetery, so I hummed instead. Tears were streaming down my face."

Cemeteries like Père Lachaise, with pastoral scenery, monuments designed by famous architects, sculptures by famous artists, and famous bodies were replicated in other countries. One of the largest was Brookwood Cemetery, which was built by the London Necropolis Company. Situated about thirty miles outside of London, Brookwood had a private railway station in London and its own trains. The sign on the railroad station at Brookwood read: Necropolis.

In the United States, the history of cemeteries in Europe was repeated. In the 1600s in America, the first European settlers

It is not uncommon to find graves clustered according to family, religion, ethnicity, and race. Surrounded by an iron fence is the Warren family plot in the Burial Ground cemetery in Plymouth, Massachusetts. It includes the grave of Mercy Otis Warren, a playwright and historian of the American Revolutionary War, and her husband, James, who was a statesman and soldier during the American Revolution. The tallest stone has a bas-relief of James on the front, and it was erected in his honor more than a hundred years after he died.

typically buried dead people in family plots on farms and plantations. But as churches were built, graveyards were created
beside them. Dead people who were prestigious, however, were
often buried inside the church—very important people were
buried under the altar, important people went under the floor of
the nave or aisles, and the minister was buried under the pulpit.
In her book, *Death in Early America*, Margaret Coffin quotes the
account of a colonial man who secretly watched a burial under
a church when he was a youngster: "The body was carried into a
dimly-lighted vault. I was so small and short, that I could see
scarcely anything. But the deep sepulchral voice of Mr. Parker
[the minister] . . . filled me with the most delightful horror. I listened and shivered. At length he uttered the words 'earth to
earth' and Grossman [the sexton] . . . rattled on the coffin a
whole shovelful of coarse gravel—'ashes to ashes'—another
shovelful of gravel—'dust to dust'—another; it seemed as if
shovel and all were cast upon the coffin lid. I never forgot it."

By the early 1800s, a chorus of complaints grew loud in America. "It is very common in this country to have churchyards in
the middle of populous cities . . . thousands of putrid carcasses,
so near the surface of the earth in a place where the air is con-
fined . . . and that such air, when breathed into the lungs must
occasion diseases. . . . Burying within churches is a practice still
more detestable . . . and renders it a very unsafe place for the living," wrote one physician. By the 1820s the cemetery cleanup
campaign started in America. Laws were passed that regulated
where bodies could be buried. Old crowded cemeteries were
closed and new ones created. Dr. Joseph Bigelow, who wanted to

Top left: *Small country cemeteries like this one in Iowa are common in the United States, but rare in Europe or Asia because land is too scarce to use for long-term storage of corpses. In some regions cemeteries are very crowded and graves are reused by digging up the remains after a set period of time and removing the bones to a storage area. Then the grave is available for a fresh corpse.* Bottom left: *Church graveyards like this one in Elizabeth, New Jersey, date back to colonial times in the northeastern United States. Today modern stores, parking lots, and office buildings surround this burial site.* Right: *Mount Auburn Cemetery in Cambridge, Massachusetts, the first "garden" or "rural" cemetery in America. The grave of Dorothea Dix, the crusader for the humane care of people with mental illness, is in the foreground.*

build a modern cemetery like Père Lachaise, and the Massachusetts Horticultural Society, which wanted to build an experimental garden, joined forces to create the first "rural" or "garden" cemetery, Mount Auburn in Cambridge, Massachusetts. The result was a spectacular cemetery with an Egyptian gate and fence that surrounded lakes, winding paths, and lush foliage. People were ecstatic, and throngs of famous and ordinary city dwellers went there to walk, meditate, and play. "Cemeteries are all the 'rage'; people lounge in them and use them (as their tastes are inclined) for walking, making love, weeping, sentimentalizing, and everything in short," an Englishman wrote after he toured Mount Auburn. Before long, rural cemeteries were built throughout the United States, including Hartford, Chicago, and San Francisco. Greenwood Cemetery in Brooklyn, New York, a rural cemetery with a harbor view, became a leading tourist attraction. At times sixty thousand people visited it a year for everything from attending funerals to taking moonlight strolls.

This section of regulation military gravestones is located in National Cemetery, Brooklyn, New York.

Today there are more than 150,000 burial places in the United States of all types and sizes: church graveyards, family plots, huge urban and small country cemeteries, and the rural style. For veterans and their immediate families there are more than a hundred military cemeteries, including the National Memorial Cemetery of the Pacific near Honolulu, Hawaii, which is cupped in a dormant volcano and known as the "Punch Bowl." The newest type of cemetery in the United States is the memorial park, or a cemetery without traditional headstones, monuments, or tombs, just memorial tablets that are flush with the ground. Hubert Eaton pioneered the concept in California and built Forest Lawn Memorial Park into "a great park, devoid of misshapen monuments and other customary signs of earthly death, but filled with towering trees, sweeping lawns, splashing fountains, singing birds, beautiful statuary, cheerful flowers." Today Forest Lawn is one of the largest cemeteries in the world. In addition to funeral facilities it has concert halls, chapels, a cinema, elaborate gardens, and more than seven hundred statues. For people who want to make a profit running a cemetery, memorial parks are less expensive to maintain than traditional cemeteries, where lawn mowers have to dodge headstones. Although most memorial parks don't even attempt to emulate Forest Lawn, they are becoming common throughout the United States. In recent years I've noticed that even traditional cemeteries often include memorial parks in sections of their grounds. There are even memorial parks on the Internet. Most plots cost less than $15 and feature e-mail tributes, photographs, and, in some cases, a recording of the dead person's voice.

Lawn mowing in spring in Brookside Cemetery, Engle-wood, New Jersey.

In most places and in all times, cemeteries have reflected differences in social standing and wealth. "The 'lower classes,' the 'hewers of wood and drawers of water' in Peru, as everywhere else, met in death a treatment corresponding with that meted out to them in life," wrote E. George Squier in his account about his explorations of the Incas. "They were thrust into holes in the nitrous sands of the coasts, or into crevices of the rocks among the mountains." In ancient Rome rich people built themselves elaborate tombs, and dead indigent people were dumped in unlined twelve-foot-square holes in the ground that were dug in Esquiline Hill. So were the bodies of some slaves, criminals, and "unidentified" dead bodies; carcasses of dead animals; and refuse from the streets. In the mid-nineteenth century in Naples, Italy, a cemetery was divided into 365 pits, a pit for every day of the year. A marble slab with a huge iron ring covered each pit. Day after day a cart loaded with unclaimed dead bodies or bodies of people who were too poor to afford a funeral

I found this gravestone in the carefully kept Linwood Cemetery, Cedar Rapids, Iowa. The superintendent of the cemetery did not have any more information about the marker.

stopped beside a pit. Workers grabbed the iron ring, lifted off the top, dumped in the bodies, threw in a load of quicklime, and replaced the top. By the time the pit was opened again, a year later on the same day, the fresh corpses would land on a bed of bones, the remains of previous years' deposits of dead bodies.

Today in the United States, corpses that are unclaimed or unidentified or that no family member or friend can afford to bury are generally buried in mass graves. In Chicago, Illinois, they are buried in groups of about thirty-five in a memorial park. In New York City they are ferried to Hart Island for burial in a mass grave. These free burial sites are typically known as potter's fields. The first burial ground referred to as a potter's field is mentioned in the book of Matthew in the New Testament in the account of when Judas returned the thirty pieces of silver that he had received for betraying Jesus Christ to the high priests of Jerusalem: "But the chief priests, taking the pieces of silver, said, 'It is not lawful to put them into the treasury, since

The Gee Poy Kuo Association of Chinese and American-born Chinese erected this arch to mark a section for their members in Greenwood Cemetery in Brooklyn, New York. Part of the inscription reads that the association "gives strength and honor to our ancestors and encourages filial piety and good conduct in our sons and daughters."

they are blood money.' So they took counsel, and bought with them the potter's field, to bury strangers in." The field, which had once been used by potters to dig clay, was probably in the Valley of Hinnom near Jerusalem. The term potter's field became widely used in the United States in the 1800s.

In addition to class differences among people, cemeteries reflect ethnic, religious, and cultural diversity. Separate cemeteries have been established for Jews, Protestants, Roman Catholics, Mormons, and Muslims. Within Evergreen Cemetery in Hillside, New Jersey, there are sections of graves of orphan children, Gypsies, Civil War soldiers, and various ethnic groups. Holy Cross Cemetery in Brooklyn, New York, is a predominantly Irish Catholic cemetery. When I visited Pioneer Cemetery in Watsonville, California, alongside the main section that contained the graves of the white settlers and their descendants, I found a Hispanic section, a Chinese section, and

This photograph shows a headstone in a section with many graves of Serbs in Rock Creek Cemetery in Washington, D.C. A picture of the Madonna and child are at the center of the Eastern Orthodox cross, and the large word at the base of the cross is written in the Cyrillic alphabet, which the Serbs use. Putting a photograph of the deceased person like the two on this headstone is a common custom in many cultures.

a Japanese section. Many separate cemeteries and separate sections were created because of people's preferences. Others, however, were created because of their prejudices. To protest segregated cemeteries in the United States, Thaddeus Stevens, a white politician who had devoted his career to abolishing slavery, decided to be buried in the "Negro" graveyard in Lancaster, Pennsylvania. Part of the inscription on his grave reads:

In the background on a knoll stands a marble statue of a nurse, eight and a half feet tall, overlooking the graves of hundreds of military nurses who are buried in Arlington National Cemetery in Arlington, Virginia.

"Finding other Cemeteries limited as to Race . . . I have chosen that I might illustrate in my death the Principles which I advocated Through a long life." Writer and folklorist Zora Neale Hurston was buried in an unmarked grave in a Negro cemetery, Garden of the Heavenly Rest, in Fort Pierce, Florida, until the writer Alice Walker found her grave and had a gravestone erected with the inscription: Zora Neale Hurston, "A Genius of the South," Novelist, Folklorist, Anthropologist, 1901–1960.

People who create cemeteries expect them to last forever. However, they don't. Cemeteries have been neglected and abandoned. They have been excavated by archaeologists. During the French Revolution, cemeteries were dug up in search of lead coffins to melt down for bullets. Other cemeteries have been covered over and turned into parks, such as Washington Square Park in New York City. Buildings and roads have also been built over old cemeteries. In 1989 construction of a beachfront hotel in Hawaii continued even after workers discovered that the site was an ancient burial ground with nine hundred skeletons. In Cairo, Egypt, the city of the dead is now the city of the living, where more than 120,000 people live in the mausoleums. Many even have electricity and telephones. Throughout the cemetery are shops, schools, small businesses, and mosques. Weddings take place there, and, of course, there are still burials.

Although most burial sites are in the ground, others are in the water. Many Hindus put cremated remains in the Ganges River, a sacred place according to their beliefs. Ancient Ethiopians disposed of corpses in their lakes. People who died onboard

A body can't be legally buried in a cemetery without a burial permit. No one can get a burial permit unless he or she has an official death certificate for the body. This burial permit was issued in Englewood, New Jersey, on April 13, 1898, for the "Burial of Two Still Born Children . . . the cause of death being Unknown."

ships were typically sewed in a hammock or piece of canvas and slid off a plank into the sea. To date, no body has been buried in space, and no one knows for sure what would happen to it. According to Kenneth Iserson, "Based on the nature of space and the factors that cause a body to decompose, however, one would suspect that a human corpse in space would decay just like any other body as long as it was sealed under an atmospheric pressure approximating that of Earth. . . . If a body were to be rapidly exposed to the near-vacuum of space, it would disintegrate or very possibly explode. If it were slowly exposed to the vacuum, it would remain in deep freeze . . . creating a freeze-dried mummy."

Before corpses end up in a cemetery or other burial site, however, they typically are the center of attention in burial rituals, some ordinary and some extraordinary.

·seven·

Rituals for People Who Have Died: Burial Customs, Ceremonies, and Celebrations

"From the time I was eight years old until I was twelve, I was one of the 'singing girls' at every funeral on Amrum, a small German island in the North Sea, where I grew up," Marlise Johnson told me. "There were ten of us. First we'd sing in the living room, where the corpse lay in an open coffin. After the minister read from the Bible and said prayers, the coffin was closed and put on a wagon. Horses pulled the wagon in a procession to the cemetery. We led the way, walking in front of the horses and singing the whole time. The immediate family walked behind the wagon. The rest of the people followed the family. It was three miles each way. I got paid the equivalent of one dollar, a lot of money especially since that was when World War II had just ended."

Throughout history and across cultures, people have performed a variety of burial customs, ceremonies, and celebrations. And they still do today. While I was writing this book, I talked with a group of international graduate students at Teachers College, Columbia University, about burial rituals in their countries and cultures. As I listened, I was fascinated and

This picture of a Turkish boy with a braid in his hair in memory of his two sisters who died was taken by photographer Lewis Hine in 1918 in Skoplie, Serbia. In other times and places hair was part of a burial ritual. In ancient Greece there was a custom of cutting a piece of children's hair and placing it in a parent's coffin. During the late 1800s in England and the United States, it was common to cut a piece of the dead person's hair and place it in a special compartment in a mourning ring or locket to be worn by a friend or relative.

inspired by the diversity and power of people's different beliefs and experiences. In Ghana, Salifu Yamusah said, "It is expected that people show respect to the memory of dead relatives. Otherwise some people believe they run the risk of forfeiting blessings that come from the dead person. To invoke the blessing of deceased relatives some people practice customs such as the pouring of libations, or drink offerings, during the long period of mourning or at the beginning of traditional ceremonies." A student from Kenya, Joyce Miano, talked about growing up in a large city where her family practiced a blend of rural African rituals and Christian practices. Pauline Manhertz, who is from Kingston, West Indies, talked about the fear of death and the fear of ghosts in her culture. "Purple is the burial color," she said. "After my stepfather's funeral, my mother refused to return to the house because it was painted purple and that might attract his ghost. Eventually she sold it."

Ojoma Edeh, who is from the Igala people in Nigeria, described the custom of burying people in layers of clothing. "My mom was buried in twenty-seven layers of clothing," she said. Ojoma explained that different family members were responsible for providing a different layer. Since her father was dead, members of his lineage carried out his responsibility to provide the layer of clothing that went against her mother's skin. As the last-born child, Ojoma was expected to provide the last layer because the last-born child is considered to be the one who loves the mother best since after that child's birth the mother didn't have to endure labor pains again. "And the top layer has to be especially expensive," Ojoma explained. According to the belief in Ojoma's culture, dead people live on in newborn children. Just before Ojoma was born, her mother's sister died. "They gave me her name and they gave me her respect. I was never spanked because I was my mom's sister," she explained, and then added with a laugh: "That's why I was so spoiled!"

During our conversations several people talked about burial rituals that involve washing and dressing the dead person, a typical practice in many times and cultures. Ishita Khemka, who is from India, described how the family carefully washes the dead person's body and dresses it in clean, cotton clothes in preparation for cremation. "For a Hindu, death is really clean. The body is washed, then it is cremated and it mingles with the wind, air, and earth," she explained. According to Aikaterini Chatzistyli, "Those who dress the dead are the most blessed in Greece. An outsider cannot do it; only a family member of the same sex as the dead person can see the naked body. As my mother's daughter, I will prepare her body when she dies."

After our conversation Aikaterini returned to Greece to visit her family and friends. When she returned, she told me: "One night we were sitting around talking, and I told people about your book and our discussion. Immediately people started telling me about this ritual and that ritual. My mother talked about putting a coin in the pocket of the dead person's clothing for the journey to heaven and Saint Peter, a custom that goes back to ancient Greece, when people used to put a coin in the dead person's mouth as payment to Charon for ferrying the ghost over the river Styx or the Acheron River to Hades. Peo-

This mask of the Dogon people in the Republic of Mali was worn by a participant in the Dama Ceremony, which was accompanied by dances and music and commemorated the dead person's transition to the realm of the ancestors.

ple were so eager to share information; it's ironic how *thanatos* [the Greek word for death] is so interesting."

Although burial rituals vary according to the historic period and culture, certain practices, in one form or another, appear in burial rituals in all times and in many cultures. One of these is the practice of washing and dressing the dead body that Ishita and Aikaterini discussed. For hundreds of years in the United States it was a custom that neighbors performed for each other. In cities some people did it for a living. In 1810 a directory in Philadelphia, Pennsylvania, listed fourteen women as "Layers Out of the Dead." Today funeral directors typically play this role. For centuries it has been an essential part of Islam and Orthodox Jewish burial rituals, and it still is today. Judy Reishtein, who is a modern Orthodox Jew, is a member of Chevra Kadisha, a group of Jews who perform the prescribed ritual of washing and dressing the *niftar*, or the one who has passed away or been relieved of life. "It is considered one good deed you do for someone with no expectation of return," Judy said.

Aisha Zikria, who is a Muslim, described her experience with burial rituals: "It's very simple. The body is put in a cool place, no refrigeration, and washed with water, herbs, and camphor. Washing the body is the most important act; it is the highest honor, and it is done by a family member. Males wash males, and females wash females. If a family member of the same sex is not available, someone is hired to wash the body. While washing the body, some prayers from the Koran are read. Then the jaw is closed with a white cloth tied around the chin, herbs are put on the eyelids, the feet are tied together, and the body is wrapped in a white cotton shroud, put in a simple coffin, just raw wood, no lining, and taken to the cemetery within twenty-four hours. At the cemetery the top is either taken off the coffin or the body is removed from the coffin totally and placed in the grave because we are told that our destiny is 'dust to dust.' The body is placed so that the head faces toward Mecca. Prayers are said throughout the burial ritual."

Of all the burial customs, one of the most widespread appears to be the practice of burying items such as tools, weapons, pottery, food, and jewelry with the dead person; people around the world from Paleolithic times to modern times have put items in graves. Known as grave goods, these items have been buried with bodies and cremated remains for several reasons, including the belief that the item would be needed in the next life. Other

In many times and places people have left objects used by the dead person on top of graves. The purpose was to pacify the dead person's spirit. This grave, which is on St. Helena Island, South Carolina, was photographed by Doris Ulmann in the late 1920s. It is probably located in Coffin Point Cemetery, which was founded in the 1800s as a burial ground for slaves. The objects include a clock, a cup, a goblet, and pots.

people believed that grave goods would pacify potential ghosts. Burying items was also a way to honor a person and express affection.

Excavations of graves have uncovered knives, axes, and other tools; mirrors and combs; food, dishes, eating utensils, cups and goblets; weapons and armor; musical instruments; beds, chairs, and other furniture; toys and games; keys and coins; and an array of jewelry, including brooches, rings, pendants, necklaces, anklets, beads, buckles, and headdresses. *Shabitis,* or carved figures of workers who would supposedly work for the dead person, were found in the graves of wealthy Egyptians. In a Hopewell Indian burial mound, archaeologists found twelve thousand pearls, thirty-five thousand pearl beads, twenty thousand shell beads, and sheets of hammered gold, copper, and iron bead. Copper figures of birds, turtles, and humans were found in another Hopewell grave. In a Viking grave in Sweden, a large number of ice skates made of the shinbone of a pig were discovered. When archaeologists uncovered the grave of the Viking queen Asa, who died in C.E. 850, they discovered that she was buried in a Viking ship along with three sleighs and a baggage sled, three beds, three chests, lamps, the contents of an entire kitchen, four looms, woven cloth and fabrics, and other items that she would need for her journey to the next world.

Another widely used burial ritual is a procession. In ancient Rome ordinary dead people had simple processions. Neighbors and friends were notified when to gather for the funeral. The sons or other close male relatives would lift the body onto their shoulders and walk to the tomb, sometimes behind a band of

Funeral Vault of Qin Shi Huang. In 212 B.C.E. the first emperor of China, Qin Shi Huang, decreed that work begin on a vast funeral vault for himself, and so hundreds of thousands of workers built an extensive subterranean tomb that was covered with earth and planted with grass to resemble a hill. When the tomb was finished, the workers were apparently entombed alive so that they wouldn't reveal information to grave robbers about the secret traps and passageways. Although it was unusual to kill so many people, sacrificing people as part of a burial ritual for rulers or very rich people was common in many ancient cultures. Typically it was wives and servants who were killed and buried with the dead person in order to provide services in the next world. In 1974 peasants who were digging a well discovered Emperor Qin Shi Huang's tomb, which contained an extraordinary sight buried fifteen to twenty feet deep under three roofed vaults—seven thousand life-size terra-cotta warrior figures. Grouped in battle formation in an honor guard for the emperor, some warriors were armed with weapons and others were mounted on horse-drawn chariots. They all had lifelike faces. The people in the photograph are cataloging and restoring the figures.

musicians. People would be summoned for the funeral procession of an extraordinary person by a public crier, who shouted:
"*Ollus Quiris leto datus. Exsequias, quibus est commodum, ire iam
tempus est. Ollus ex aedibus effertur,*" or, "This citizen has surren-
dered to death. For those who find it convenient, it is now time
to attend the funeral. He is being brought from his house." A
band of musicians would definitely lead this funeral procession.
It also might include people singing dirges in praise of the dead
person and groups of buffoons and jesters, who would entertain
the bystanders, perhaps with imitations of the deceased. Next in
line were actors wearing the wax masks of the dead person's

*A funeral procession in
Ponce, Puerto Rico, with
older children carrying the coffin of a child, January 1938.*

ancestors; on some occasions hundreds of masks were displayed. The corpse, with its face uncovered, carried aloft on a couch, came next, followed by the family. Friends, slaves, and freedmen, or former slaves, were next. Everyone wore mourning garb and openly expressed their grief. Regardless of the time of day, torchbearers accompanied the procession.

Funeral processions are as diverse as the people of the world. In the burial rituals of the Australian Bushmen, mourners are painted with white clay and the bleached bones of the dead person are carried in a tree trunk. In Venice, Italy, gondolas carry the coffin and the mourners in the funeral procession, which crosses the water to the cemetery island of San Michele. The funeral processions of the Amish people in the United States are made up of horse-drawn carriages. Gus Feaster, who was a former slave in South Carolina, left an oral history about his life as a slave. According to Feaster, "Goin' to funerals we used all Marse's wagons. Quick as de funeral start, de preacher give out a funeral hymn. All in de procession took up de tune and as de wagons move along with de mules at a slow walk, everybody sing dat hymn. When it was done, another was lined out, and dat kept up till we reach de graveyard. Then de preacher pray and we sung some mo'. . . . On de way home from de funeral, de mules would perk up a little in dey walk and a faster hymn was sung on de way home. When we got home, we was in a good mood from singing de faster hymns and de funeral soon be forgot."

Beginning in the early 1800s in some southern cities in the United States, especially in New Orleans, Louisiana, funeral

This coffin with the remains of Judge Humes arrived in Valdez, Alaska, from Fairbanks by dogsled.

processions featured a brass band. "On the way to the cemetery it was customary for the band to play very slowly and mournfully a dirge, or a Protestant hymn such as *Nearer My God to Thee*, but on the way back the band would strike up a lively spiritual such as *When the Saints Go Marching In*, or a ragtime song such as *Oh, Didn't He Ramble*, or a syncopated march," Eileen Southern writes in her book *The Music of Black America: A History*. The band typically included two to three cornets, two trombones, an alto horn, a baritone horn, a tuba, one to two clarinets, and a snare drum and bass drum, and during the exuberant return trip mourners invited passersby to join the procession. Over the years many tourists went to New Orleans, checked the local newspaper for the daily listing of funeral parades, and went to watch, even participate. Today, however, funeral parades are rare.

When kings and queens die, they usually have elaborate processions, as did King Rama VI of Thailand when he died in 1926. First the king's corpse was washed, dressed in elegant clothes, and briefly displayed on a bier, or a stand on which a corpse, coffin, or casket is placed. Then it was folded up with the knees drawn up under the chin and inserted in a large golden urn. After a waiting period, the urn with the remains was taken to be cremated on a pyre, a magnificent structure with columns, carved wood, and a cone-shaped roof. In their book *Celebrations of Death*, Richard Huntington and Peter Metcalf described the funeral procession to the pyre: "Troops . . . 160 red drums of victory . . . 28 blowers of the Siamese bugles, 4 blowers of conch shells, 2 seven tiered umbrellas . . . the GREAT FUNERAL CAR, bearing the urn, and drawn by 200 soldiers and six royal horses, a royal umbrella, sunshade and fan . . . THE KING (new one), walking, . . . representatives of foreign states . . . military units with bands."

Many cultures have burial rituals that involve never leaving the body alone until it is buried. This vigil has been called a wake and for some people it is a way to comfort the spirit of the dead person. Other people believe that they are protecting the dead person from evil spirits, and, in some regions, animals. According to Randall M. Miller and John David Smith in their

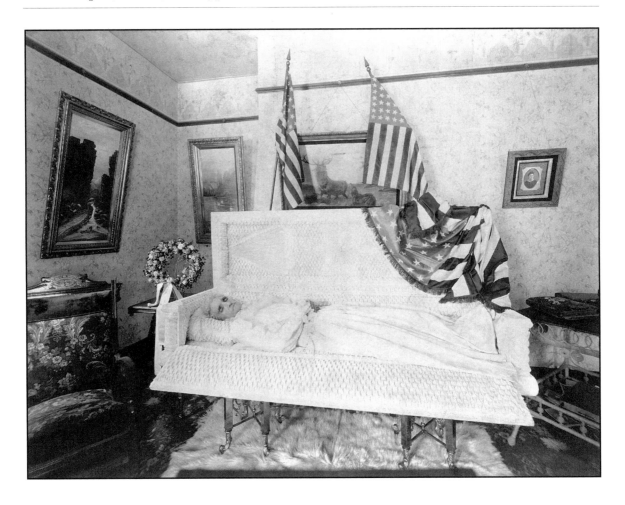

Lying in state, or putting a dead body on public display with pomp and ceremony, is typically reserved for rulers, heads of state, and prominent citizens like Mrs. Colby Suther, who died in Muncie, Indiana, in 1898.

book *Dictionary of Afro-American Slavery,* "In the semitropical heat of Southern and Caribbean plantations, corpses quickly decayed and the slave community had to protect the dead from prowling cats and other animals. From Virginia to Louisiana, from South Carolina to Barbados, the slaves would 'sit up' all night with the dead, singing and praying through the night." Of course, in the days when premature burial was a real concern, a wake was also a sensible way to watch for signs of life.

In the United States today, a wake usually means a time at a funeral home when friends and acquaintances can visit the family and pay respects to the dead person, who is in either a closed or an open coffin. Traditionally in the United States, dead bodies were laid out at home. In the late 1800s, in brownstones, or tall, narrow houses that are attached to each other, coffin corners, or niches, were typically cut in the walls of narrow stairway landings to allow turning room when coffins were carried up and down. When she was a child in 1942, Hedy Leutner remembers going to a wake in a home for one of her fourth-grade classmates. "There were flowers on the front door tied with a black ribbon. My friend's coffin was in the living room. She was in it, wearing her white first communion dress."

Death typically involves mourning and many burial rituals have to do with managing grief. In ancient Egypt, when the male head of the household died, the women were expected to rush through the streets as they beat their breasts, periodically grabbed their hair, and wailed. Since ancient times Jews have made a tear in their clothes on hearing that someone close to them has died. "It allows the mourner to give vent to pent-up anger and anguish," Maurice Lamn writes in his book *The Jewish Way in Death and Mourning*. Hindus limit the time they mourn because they believe that grieving holds the dead person's soul back from its journey. However, in some ancient and modern cultures, it has been so important to have a large number of mourners that people made a living selling their services as professional mourners. In colonial America mourners expected to receive gifts when they attended funerals—rings, scarves, and gloves. In 1738, at the funeral of Andrew Faneuil in Boston, over three thousand pairs of gloves were given away, despite laws that had been passed in 1721 and 1724 by the General Court of Massachusetts prohibiting "extraordinary expense at funerals."

In addition to expressing grief and giving gifts, mourning rituals sometimes include certain colors—black in many modern western cultures, light blue for Armenians and Syrians, and white for Hindus and Chinese; trees—cypress in Greece, sakaki in Japan, and weeping willow in the United States; and flowers—chrysanthemums in Italy, marigolds in Mexico, and mandrakes, a perennial plant with purplish-and-white flowers that Germans make into dolls and put in caskets. In the modern-day United States mourning rituals are generally downplayed. People no longer put black wreaths on their doors or wear black armbands like they used to. However, based on my research, one American custom continues unchanged—bringing lots of food to grieving families, which is one of my most vivid memories from when my brother died—food, food, food. As the word

Burial sites have been marked in a wide variety of ways. This is a postcard of an Eskimo grave marker.

The labels in the photograph read: "TABLE WHERE SHE WAS LAID", "SISTER'S SEAT", "THE WAY I HELD HER", "COPYRIGHT 1915 BY STINCHCOMB PHOTO STUDIO", "NOT LOST", "BUT GONE", "BEFORE"

"Not Lost But Gone Before." *During the late 1800s and early 1900s, many Americans had a sentimental fascination with death. During this time maudlin poetry about dead children and ghost stories were popular. Etiquette books described the proper rules about how to conduct funerals and mourn. Wearing mourning jewelry was fashionable, including rings engraved with the dead person's name and lockets with a piece of the dead person's hair. So were mourning pictures like this one of a family in Greshamville, Georgia. The title printed at the bottom is "Not Lost But Gone Before," and the upheld hands indicate the family's belief in heaven. The other labels from left to right are "The way I held her," "Sister's seat," "Table where she was laid [in her coffin]."*

spread in our small town that my brother had died, friends showed up with hams, turkeys, casseroles, breads, cookies, cakes, and pies. Food has been a part of burial rituals in all times and cultures. People buried food and drink with the dead person and left it on the grave. In many cultures it is common for people to gather at someone's house and eat together after the funeral. Roberta Halporn, executive director of the Center for Thanatology, gave me this recipe for a pie known as Funeral Pie because it is so easy to make that it was commonly served at postfuneral meals in some parts of the United States:

Funeral Pie

Pastry for two-crust nine-inch pie

2 cups raisins

1 cup orange juice

1 cup water

¾ cup plus one tablespoon sugar

2 tablespoons cornstarch

1 teaspoon allspice

½ cup chopped walnuts or other nuts

1 tablespoon lemon juice

Preheat oven to 425 degrees and line a pie pan with half the pastry. Combine the raisins, orange juice, and water in a saucepan. Bring to a boil. Reduce heat and let simmer for five minutes. Combine ¼ cup sugar, cornstarch, and allspice and stir into the raisin mixture. Cook, stirring until thickened, about one minute. Stir in nuts and lemon juice. Pour filling into the prepared pie pan. Cover with the top crust and flute the edges. Brush the top of the pie with a little beaten egg. Sprinkle with the remaining tablespoon of sugar. Put pie in oven and bake twenty to twenty-five minutes or until the crust is golden and the filling bubbly. Let cool slightly before serving. Serve with ice cream or whipped cream.

Some burial rituals happen long after a person died. "Winter is also the corpse-turning season," Dervla Murphy writes in her book about Madagascar. "During these exhumation ceremonies corpses are removed from their tombs, wrapped in new shrouds

This is what it cost to bury my stepgrandmother in 1975, including cremation charges. Today crematory charges range from $150 to $475, while the average funeral in which the person is not cremated costs about $4,700.

LAZEAR-SMITH FUNERAL HOME, INC.

PHONE (AREA CODE 914) 986-4331
IF NO ANSWER (914) 986-4466

17 OAKLAND AVENUE
WARWICK, NEW YORK 10990

Estate of Greta Leskovar
Care of Mr. Joseph Leskovar
169 West St.
Warwick, N.Y.

Professional Services, including preparation of the deceased, the use of Funeral Home and Equipement, arranging and direction of the Funeral, use of Funeral Coach and Casket as selected. $ 660.00

Cash Advanced by the Funeral Home
Crematory Charges $ 90.00
Three Certified Transcripts   6.00   96.00

Balance $ 756.00

Paid In Full
May 12, 1975
Thank you
Wilbur F. Smith

and often made guests of honour at jolly parties in their descendants' homes, before being returned to the spring-cleaned tombs with gifts of money and alcohol. This custom may startle when first encountered, yet to condemn it as 'morbid' is to miss the point. The Malagasy experience such a vivid sense of unity with the dead that maintaining contact with their corpses seems only natural—a recognition of their being alive and well and very powerful in the Ankoatra, 'the Beyond.' "

Other postburial rituals include a "second burial," or a memorial service that was held when it was believed the dead person's spirit had reached its destination and was at rest. A common custom in West Africa, "second burials" were also practiced by slaves in the United States. For Jews postburial rituals include "three days of deep grief, seven days of mourning (or *shivah*), thirty days of gradual readjustment, and eleven months of

Throughout Mexico and many parts of the United States, roadside crosses mark the spot of fatal accidents. Friends and relatives take care of the crosses and redecorate them each year. The cross at the curve in this photograph is located on Route 78 in California.

remembrance and healing," writes Audrey Gordon in *Jewish Reflections on Death.*

One of several postburial rituals for Roman Catholics is to celebrate memorial masses for people on the anniversary of their death date. Roman Catholics also celebrate the Days of the Dead, official holidays in the Catholic calendar. In C.E. 834 Pope Gregory IV established November 1 as All Saints' Day, a day to celebrate dead saints. The date was selected to coincide with an ancient festival of the dead that the Celts had practiced before they became Christians. The mass for All Saints' Day was called Allhollowmas. In time, the evening before became known as All Hallow e'en, or Halloween. In the fourteenth century November 2 was established as All Souls' Day, a day to celebrate all dead people. Today a variety of celebrations take place on both days, especially in Roman Catholic countries.

In Mexico November 2 is known as Día los Muertos, or the Day of the Dead. By mid-October bakeries and markets are stocked with *pan de muerto,* or "bread of the dead." These loaves are often decorated with meringues fashioned into different shapes, including bones. People give gifts of colorful sugar skulls with names inscribed on them and write *calaveras,* or verses with witty allusions to death or epitaphs. On the day itself, families go to the graveyards. They decorate the graves with marigolds, the flower of the dead, burn incense, and have picnics that include the dead person's favorite foods and drinks. The celebrations last all day and end with prayers and chants for the dead.

My brother and father had traditional Protestant funeral services. There was a three-day wake and a service in a church led

This handcrafted metal skeleton is seated on a couch that was made from a cast-iron stovepipe. It was made to be placed on a home altar during the Day of the Dead celebration in Mexico.

by a minister. The service included a eulogy, music, Scripture readings, and prayers, a typical funeral for many Americans. As for Willi, Frieda and I carried his urn to the cemetery in Koryčany, the Czech Republic. We had arrived two days earlier, and I had already visited the cemetery, which was beautifully maintained by the villagers, who made weekly and sometimes daily visits to tend to their family graves. Ruda, Frieda's brother-in-law, came with us, pulling a cart with Willi's urn, a bouquet of daffodils and a funeral wreath with a black ribbon, and a crowbar to lift the top off the grave. At the cemetery Ruda and I and a friend of Ruda's grunted and sweated as we used the crowbar to remove the marble slab. Then we set Willi's urn next to urns of other family members and wrestled the cover back in place. A few tears rolled down Frieda's cheek. I put my arm around her and briefly talked about Willi's exuberant smile. Leaning on the crowbar, Ruda said a few words in Czech. We arranged the wreath and daffodils, stood silently for a time, and then walked away.

Before Grammie's funeral in Randolph Center, Vermont, my aunt had called me to remind me that they were atheists and therefore did not want any formal service or a minister involved. "She's just going to end up 'dust to dust,' just like the dust balls under the bed," she said. When I told her that Grammie had asked me to read her favorite Bible verses, she said, "Well, anyone who comes can just do whatever they want." And that is exactly what happened. Standing around Grammie's grave, over which her coffin rested on a device that would be used to lower it into the hole after we finished, we all did our

Willi Matousek's Burial at Koryčany. Willi Matousek's cremated remains were buried in a grave in a cemetery in Koryčany, the Czech Republic. The people from left to right are Milena Berka, Frieda Matousek, Rudolf (Ruda) Berka (Frieda's brother-in-law and Milena's father), and a friend. Frieda was born Bedřišeka Žalčík, and this is her family's plot. She became Frieda when she immigrated to the United States and an immigration official renamed her because he couldn't pronounce Bedřiseka, a not uncommon immigrant experience. She became Matousek when she married Willi. Ruda is lifting up the marble top so that we can put the urn with Willi's cremated remains in a cement container that was built above the coffins of Frieda's brother, Ladislaw; mother, Antonie; and father, Cyril. My mother's father, Joseph Leskovar, and Frieda were second cousins. Another level of relationship was added after my mother's mother died at a young age and Joseph married Frieda's sister Greta.

own thing—my uncle made a speech; my sister-in-law read "Ode on a Grecian Urn," by John Keats; one of my cousins sang; another told a story about Grammie buying her a pair of red boots; I read the 23rd and 108th Psalms; and my mother and sister placed a huge bouquet of wildflowers on Grammie's coffin. Although cemetery workers typically lower the casket into the grave after the family leaves (a cemetery regulation and/or state law in some places), a few of us waited. "Hey," one of the workers said to my children, "do you want to help us lower your grandmother? You can help us turn the crank." And they did, being very careful around the open grave.

The mix of burial rituals—traditional and nontraditional—in my family is becoming more common in the United States. Although some people continue to perform traditional burial rituals, other people are creating new ones that reflect their beliefs and needs. However, regardless of the burial rituals we perpetuate or create, regardless of our age, sex, race, ethnicity, sexual orientation, and degree of disability, we are all seeking the same thing—burial rituals that help us understand and cope with the death, just as our ancestors have always done.

·eight·

Death Is Everywhere: Images in the Arts and Everyday Life

Several years after my father died, Maritza Morgan, my mother and a well-known artist, completed a painting of the biblical character Lazarus. As the story appears in the Bible, Lazarus had been dead for four days when Jesus resurrected him: "Then Jesus, deeply moved again, came to the tomb; it was a cave, and a stone lay upon it. Jesus said, 'Take away the stone.' Martha, the sister of the dead man, said to him, 'Lord, by this time there will be an odor, for he has been dead four days.' Jesus said to her, 'Did I not tell you that if you would believe you would see the glory of God?' So they took away the stone. And Jesus lifted up his eyes and said, 'Father, I thank thee that thou hast heard me. . . .' When he had said this, he cried with a loud voice, 'Lazarus, come out!' The dead man came out."

My mother's painting was of the dead Lazarus with his family and friends. When I first saw the painting, I was startled to see familiar faces and body shapes: the dead Lazarus stretched out in the foreground was my father—his head, features, and emaciated body that had been ravaged by cancer for three years before he died. The woman sitting beside him and holding his head

The painting Lazarus *that my mother, Maritza Morgan (1920–1997), painted after my father's death, 1969. Carving, acrylic, and gold leaf on wood, 22½ × 40".*

looked like my mother. I recognized family friends—Chaim and Hildegard Zemach, Francesca Goodell Rappole—standing in the background. I was there too, with my family and our white dog. My brothers, Kip and Vin, were there. My sister, Cam, was holding three orange flowers with greenish yellow centers. The painting was undeniably powerful, although it was painful to see my father's dead body so vividly portrayed. But I understood that my mother had done what people have done in all times and all places—she had joined death and art.

Neolithic people created wall paintings of burial rituals. The ancient Egyptians painted mummy cases and tombs with hieroglyphs, religious images, magic symbols, and scenes of everyday life with people working, eating, playing, and attending ceremonies. In Japan, from the third to the seventh century, people made clay funerary sculptures to place in the burial mounds. For a time in ancient China, huge statues were placed along the road that led to an emperor's tomb. Early Christians painted portraits of saints and religious scenes in the catacombs. The Zapotec people who lived in southern Mexico made urns with ornately modeled figures with feathered headdresses and ornaments. Death and art have been joined together in making masks and totem poles. In Africa wood-carvers made ancestor figures as a place where the spirit of the dead person could live. In many different cultures corpses were buried in beautifully carved and decorated sarcophagi, tombs, coffins, and urns. The rural cemeteries in Europe and the United States were showcases for works by famous architects, sculptors, and artists. In the late twentieth century, people in the United States have made a quilt in memory of people who died from AIDS and painted graffiti in memory of people who were killed by guns.

It isn't always possible to know why people have joined death and art, but some people believed that the art helped dead people in the next world. Other people believed that it was a way to

The use of stone animals at tombs in China dates back to the Han dynasty (206 B.C.E.–220 B.C.E.) This is a picture of the animals that line the road leading to the Ming Tombs in Beijing, where thirteen of the sixteen emperors of the Ming dynasty (1368–1644) are buried. Known as the "Spirit's Road for the Mausoleum in Common" and also as the "Sacred Way," this road, it was believed, would lead the spirit home to its final resting place. There are six types of animals—real and fantasy. Two pairs face each other across the road, with the first pair sitting and the second standing, in this order: lion, hsieh-chai, camel, elephant, ch'i-lin, and horse. Just beyond the animals the road turns east to prevent the evil spirits, who were believed to travel in straight lines, from disturbing the dead.

While I was photographing this piece of contemporary urban memorial art on the side of a building in the South Bronx, New York, I met Charisse Broome, who told me that it was for David Torres. He was twenty-one years old when he was shot to death at that street corner in January 1994. "He was my best friend," she said. "We grew up together." Flanked by musical notes are large letters that spell Dave. *The epitaph in the upper-right-hand corner reads: "Be of good cheer about death and know this of truth, nothing can happen to a good man either in life or after death." The artist signed his piece "By Gear" in the lower left-hand corner.*

honor dead people. It was also a way to perpetuate certain beliefs. In the late 1500s, when the plague was ravaging the populations of Europe, priests began putting drawings on church walls in which a skeleton was leading a procession of people—workers, beggars, monks, royalty, and the Pope. The skeleton generally had a grin and was usually wearing a crown. Known as the Danse Macabre, or Dance of Death, the drawings were intended to warn sinners to repent before death came to take them away. People have also joined death and art as a way of making a moral or political statement. Jacques-Louis David, a leading French painter who supported the French Revolution, painted pictures that became very popular and inspired revolutionary feelings in France. The German artist Käthe Kollwitz created lithographs, woodcuts, and sculptures of dying and grieving people, especially children and mothers, as an expression of her protests against social injustice and war.

A scene from one of the countless representations of the Danse Macabre, or Dance of Death, that first appeared in the early 1500s in France and then spread through Europe. The idea of a procession or dance in which both living and dead people participated appeared in paintings on wood, stone, or canvas; in stained glass windows; as sculptures; in embroideries and tapestries; as engravings on stone or metal; in woodcuts; and in poems and prose. The procession of living and dead figures symbolized the idea that everyone dies regardless of their power or wealth.

By the mid-1800s, in the United States people started memorializing dead relatives with daguerreotypes, the first type of photographs. According to Gay Culverhouse, who owns a unique collection of "dead baby" daguerreotypes, "Families had pictures taken of dead family members, especially babies. It was part of the mourning ritual. The daguerreotype was mounted inside a 3″ × 3½″ finely tooled leather case. The inside was lined with burgundy or blue cut velvet and the daguerreotype was mounted inside a gold, filigreed frame. Families cherished these pictures as a way to remember and honor a dead child."

Death has been recorded by many photographers for many reasons. In the 1970s, Mark and Dan Jury photographed their grandfather's dying, death, and funeral and published the photographs in a book titled *Gramp* as a record of their love for him. Some thirty years earlier, Margaret Bourke-White, a World War II photographer for the military and *Life* magazine, entered the

A daguerreotype of a dead child.

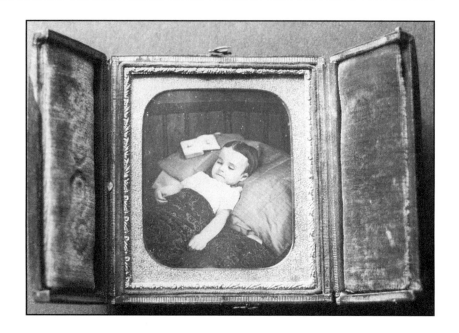

concentration camps and took many pictures of the horror that she saw, including piles of emaciated corpses. These pictures were later published in *The Living Dead of Buchenwald*. At the time she wrote, "Even though I did not realize how soon people would disbelieve or forget, I had a deep conviction that an atrocity like this demanded to be recorded."

Death has been joined with literature. "It's a theme that has preoccupied many authors and intrigues readers of all ages," says Sandie Walters, an English teacher for more than thirty years in a large urban high school. Sandie's list of examples includes "*The Odyssey*, by Homer, in which Odysseus visits the land of the dead; *The Pigman*, by Paul Zindel, which explores adolescent views on graveyards and death; *Bridge to Terabithia*, by Katherine Paterson, which deals with the death of a child and loss of a friend; William Shakespeare's play *Julius Caesar*, with its eulogy scene, *Romeo and Juliet* and the burial in the catacombs, and the supernatural phenomena in *Macbeth* and *Hamlet*; Edgar Allen Poe's depiction of unusual disposals of bodies in 'The Tell-Tale Heart' and 'The Cask of Amontillado'; and death rituals that are portrayed in *Beowulf*, the anonymous epic poem from about the eighth century, *Lord of the Flies*, by William Golding, and *The Lottery*, by Shirley Jackson."

Of course, Sandie's list is just a beginning. I remember being assigned to read William Cullen Bryant's meditation on death, *Thanatopsis*; Dante Alighieri's exploration of life after death in the *Divine Comedy*; a play, *Our Town*, by Thornton Wilder, which takes place in a cemetery; and *Elegy Written in a Country Churchyard*, by Thomas Gray, with the famous line, "The paths of glory lead but to the grave." On my own I discovered other books that dealt with death and all its dimensions: *Death Comes for the Archbishop*, by Willa Cather; *Beloved* and *Jazz*, by Toni Morrison; *The Woman Warrior: Memoir of a Girlhood Among Ghosts*, by Maxine Hong Kingston; *Paula*, by Isabel Allende;

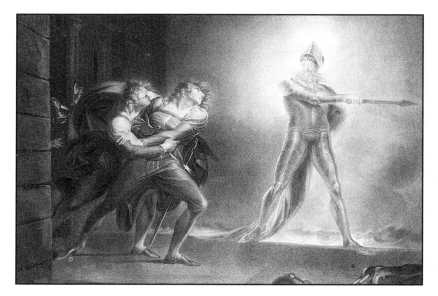

William Shakespeare's famous play Hamlet *deals with many aspects of death, including corpses, grief, gravediggers, and one of the most famous ghosts in literature—the ghost of Hamlet's father. In this picture an artist depicted (left to right) Hamlet, Horatio, Marcellus, and the ghost on the platform before the castle of Elsinore (act 1, scene 4).*

and *After a Great Pain*, by Diane Cole; a short story, "The Management of Grief," by Bharati Mukherjee; and the many poems on death by Emily Dickinson, one of which begins with the line "I heard a Fly buzz—when I died—".

Death and music have been joined too. Many burial rituals involve music. At funerals in Scotland, clans play their own laments, which are generally bagpipe pieces but sometimes songs. In the United States, funerals today often include classical music such as "The Funeral March" from the third move-

The cover of music that was composed by W. J. Robjohn after President Abraham Lincoln was assassinated.

ment of Piano Sonata no. 2 in B-flat Minor, opus 35, by Frédéric Chopin, and "For the Mountains Shall Depart," from *Elijah*, by Felix Mendelssohn. The theme music of Franco Zefferelli's 1969 movie adaptation of *Romeo and Juliet* is also played. Slaves in the United States sang spirituals at wakes and funerals. In his book *Black Song: The Forge and the Flame*, John Lovell, Jr., writes, "Death causes wake songs and hanging crepe. A famous wake song is 'Sim-me (See me here), yuh muh leaduh / All roun' duh body, sim-me yuh . . . de crepe keep a-hangin' on somebody's doorbell. . . .'" During the Civil War, funerals for Confederate officers usually included the "Dead March" from *Saul*, by George Frederick Handel. On July 21, 1862, in Richmond, Virginia, Mary Chestnut wrote in her diary, "It seems we are never out of the sound of the Dead March in *Saul*. It comes and it comes . . ."

Drums and gongs are an integral part of funerals for the Berawan, a group of people in Borneo. In the village of Long Jegan, Berawans sing a death song that provides detailed instructions to the soul about how to make the journey to the land of the dead. According to Richard Huntington and Peter Metcalf, "Eventually, in the song, the soul arrives at the mouth of the Lamat stream, and instead of passing by, it is instructed to enter. From the Lamat it goes into the Meta, a yet smaller watercourse. This route would bring one to the highest point in the neighboring mountain range. In this region, the soul is told to get out of the canoe, and to search for *sirih*, the leaves used in chewing betel. At this juncture, the death song sequence of Long Jegan abruptly terminates. It is thought that while the soul is searching for *sirih* leaves it will be discovered by emissaries from the land of the dead, who will conduct it on the remaining part of the journey. The whole recital has lasted six to eight hours, and dawn is close."

In addition to being part of burial rituals, music and death are joined by musicians, who, like artists and writers, are seeking to understand and cope with death. In honor of people who have died, many composers have written requiems, or musical versions of the Roman Catholic Mass for the Dead. In the *Messa da Requiem*, written by Giuseppe Verdi in 1874 on the death of the poet Alessandro Manzoni, the chorus sings, "*Requiem aeternam dona eis, Domine: et lux perpetua luceat eis*," or, "Eternal rest grant them, O Lord, and let perpetual light shine upon them." In 1991, when Eric Clapton's young child died, Clapton expressed his grief by writing and singing "Tears in Heaven," a song that became a big hit. After John Lennon was murdered, Elton John recorded the song "Empty Garden," which he and Bernie

Grenville Dean Wilson was an American composer. When he died, his grave was marked with a huge hunk of granite. Mounted to it was this bronze plaque. The musical notation is from one of Wilson's compositions. The quotation is from Julius Caesar *by William Shakespeare. Just below "1931" in the lower right-hand corner is the line "Janet Scudder Sc (stonecarver) 1898." Oak Hill Cemetery, Nyack, New York.*

In the last twenty years, gravestone rubbing, or copying the design and lettering from a gravestone onto a piece of paper, has become popular in the United States. According to Roberta Halporn, who is pictured here doing a rubbing, she feels a connection when she does a rubbing "to the person who is buried below and the artisan who made the monument."

Taupin wrote. After her manager and members of her band were killed in an airplane crash, Reba McEntire released an album titled *For My Broken Heart.* In dealing with the overwhelming death rate among people who live in the inner city, many artists have written hip-hop music that has been called "rap requiem," including "Tha Crossroads," by Bone Thugs-n-Harmony.

In music that deals with death, the lyrics express disparate feelings—sadness, heartbreak, anger, disbelief, and sometimes relief that a person's pain has ended. So do sounds and rhythms—the wail of a saxophone, the muffled beat of a drum, the swelling chords of an organ, the hard and driving beat of rap, trumpets playing taps, and a band in New Orleans that is cheering up mourners and sending a dead soul on its final journey.

In one way or another, death is joined with every aspect of life. Dying people and corpses, morgues and coffins, funerals and cemeteries are themes and settings in movies and on television. The daily news media frequently features stories and photographs about death. Death and dead people are the subject of jokes and cartoons. Our everyday language includes expressions such as "scared to death," "dead tired," "dead cold," "dead broke," "you're a dead duck," "drop dead," "dying to meet you," "I nearly died," "to die for," "do or die," "graveyard shift," "turning over in his or her grave," "skeleton crew," "white as a ghost," and "quiet as a tomb."

It is impossible to ignore death, even if we would like to, and even when we use euphemisms to refer to death—passed away, passed, gone for good, bit the dust, iced, bellied up, checked out, kicked the bucket, and gave up the ghost. Regardless of what we call it—death is still death. But fortunately people in all times and places have created an infinite variety of images, ideas, sights, and sounds to help us deal with death as we live our lives.

"When I Die . . ."

Although most people didn't leave instructions about what they wanted to have happen after they died, some people did. The following excerpts are a small and diverse sample of people's final requests:

Ellen Glasgow, a U.S. novelist and winner of the Pulitzer Prize, was a lifelong dog lover. Glasgow requested that two of her dogs be disinterred from their graves in her garden and be reburied with her in her coffin. They were.

The English philosopher, economist, and jurist Jeremy Bentham made this request: "My body I give to my dear-friend Doctor Southwood Smith to be disposed of in the manner hereinafter mentioned. . . . The skeleton he will cause to be put together in such manner as that the whole figure may be seated in a chair usually occupied by me when living in the attitude in which I am sitting when engaged in thought in the course of the time employed in writing. . . . He will cause the skeleton to be clad in one of the suits of black occasionally worn by me. The body so clothed together with the chair and the staff in my later years borne by me he will take charge of and for containing the

whole apparatus he will cause to be prepared an appropriate box or case and will cause to be engraved in conspicuous characters on a plate to be affixed thereon and also on the labels of the glass case in which the preparations of the soft parts of my body shall be contained . . . my name. . . . If it should so happen that my personal friends and other disciples should be disposed to meet together on some day or days of the years . . . my executor will from time to time cause to be conveyed to the room in which they meet the said Box or case with the content."

Bentham's request was followed and today his skeleton, dressed in his own suit, sits in a case in University College, London. Twice a year the Bentham Society meets for dinner, and the remains of Jeremy Bentham are removed from his case and placed at the head of the table.

The French poet Alfred de Musset expressed his request in a poem:

> *My dear friends, when I am dead*
> *Plant a willow at the cemetery,*
> *I love its weeping foliage,*
> *Its pallor is sweet and dear to me,*
> *And its shadow will be light*
> *Upon the earth where I sleep.*

De Musset was buried at Père Lachaise, and his friends planted a willow. Unfortunately willows don't thrive in the soil at the cemetery. After the American author Willa Cather visited the grave, she wrote: "De Musset certainly never got any-

Opposite: Clyde A. Chamberlin sent me the photograph of this gravestone in Scippio Cemetery near Harlan, Indiana, with the following explanation: "Archie A. 'Binkie' Arnold was a practical joker. He was a plumber by trade. He had nothing to do with parking meters. In fact, he disliked parking meters so much that he refused to put money in them and ended up with a stack of parking tickets. After Arnold's death in an automobile accident, it was revealed that he had purchased two obsolete parking meters. In his will Arnold requested that the parking meters be painted black, the reading set at Expired, indicating that his time had finally run out, the coin slot welded shut so that no one could change the reading, and the parking meters mounted on either side of his gravestone. And there they are!"

thing that he wanted in life, and it seems a sort of fine-drawn irony that he should not have the one poor willow he wanted for his grave."

Jawaharlal Nehru, first prime minister of India after independence, made this request: "When I die, I should like my body to be cremated. If I die in a foreign country, my body should be cremated there and my ashes sent to Allahabad. A small handful of these ashes should be thrown into the Ganga. . . . No part of these ashes should be retained or preserved. . . . The major portion of my ashes . . . should . . . be carried high up into the air in an aeroplane and scattered from that height over the fields where the peasants of India toil, so that they might mingle with the dust and soil of India and become an indistinguishable part of India." Nehru's request was followed.

When Franklin Delano Roosevelt was president of the United States, he wrote detailed instructions for his funeral if he died while he was "in office as the President of the United States." Roosevelt's requests included:

That a service of the utmost simplicity be held in the East Room of the White House.

That there be no lying in state anywhere.

That a gun-carriage and not a hearse be used throughout.

That the casket be of absolute simplicity, dark wood, that the body be not embalmed or hermetically sealed, and that the grave be not lined with brick, cement, or stones.

Roosevelt put the instructions in his private safe, but they weren't found until after he was buried. Of Roosevelt's requests, the only one that was followed was that there was no lying in state. His wife, Eleanor Roosevelt, vetoed that because, "We have talked often, when there had been a funeral at the Capitol in which a man had lain in state and the crowds had gone by the open coffin, of how much we disliked the practice; and we had made up our minds that we would never allow it." Apparently they hadn't discussed the other ideas because Roosevelt was embalmed, put in a fancy bronze-colored copper coffin that was bolted and sealed with cement, carried to the burial site in a hearse, and placed in a cement vault.

As part of her final request, Susan B. Anthony, a woman suffrage leader in the United States, wrote, "Remember that I want there should be no tears. Pass on, and go on with the work." Anthony died in 1906, and her colleagues heeded her words and worked until women won the right to vote with the ratification of the Nineteenth Amendment in 1920.

Born Joseph Hillstrom, Joe Hill was a Swedish-American labor organizer and songwriter for the Industrial Workers of the World (IWW). After being convicted on circumstantial evidence for murder, Hill was sentenced to be executed. The night before he was killed by a firing squad, Hill wrote his final request and handed it through the bars of his cell to the guard. Joe Hill's request has become a prized piece of poetry in the heritage of the American labor movement:

> *My will is easy to decide,*
> *For there is nothing to divide.*
> *My kin don't need to fuss and moan—*
> *'Moss does not cling to a rolling stone.'*
> *My body? Ah, If I could choose,*
> *I would to ashes it reduce,*
> *And let the merry breezes blow*
> *My dust to where some flowers grow.*
> *Perhaps some fading flowers then*
> *Would come to life and bloom again.*
> *This is my last and final will.*

Good luck to all of you,
Joe Hill

Thousands of people attended two funerals for Hill, one in Salt Lake City and one in Chicago. As he requested, his body was cremated and the leaders of the IWW divided the cremated remains into small envelopes that had Hill's picture on one side and his "last will" on the other. The envelopes containing instructions to scatter the remains were sent to people in South America, Europe, Asia, South Africa, Australia, New Zealand, and every state in the United States except Utah because Joe had said that he "didn't want to be found dead" there.

The Italian opera composer Guiseppe Verdi left strict instructions that there was to be no public display of any type at his funeral. Nevertheless, more than one hundred thousand people lined the route as Verdi's coffin was taken to a cemetery in Milan and put in an ornate marble tomb.

The American poet Emily Dickinson's final directions were carried out: her casket was white; her sister placed two heliotropes in her casket; a bunch of blue violets was at her throat and a wreath of blue violets was on her casket; she was laid out in the hall of the Homestead, the house where she was born and lived her life; and six of the Homestead's workers carried her casket out the back door, through the garden, then through the barn, and across the field to the family plot. As they walked they kept the casket in sight of the Homestead, as Dickinson had requested.

Before Jessica Mitford died in 1996, she was working on a

revised edition of *The American Way of Death*. The night before Mitford's death, her family and a few close friends, including Maya Angelou, sang her favorite songs to her—dance hall tunes, big band tunes, and a ditty, "The Ballad of Grace Darling," which tells the story about an English lighthouse keeper's daughter who saves a "shipwreck'd crew." As part of her funeral, Mitford's family arranged a funeral procession led by six horses pulling a hearse. Each horse had a black plume attached to the top of its bridle. It seems that Mitford had once said that she would like to have plumed horses pulling a hearse, a popular nineteenth-century funeral custom in Europe. A band playing "When the Saints Go Marching In" followed behind the hearse. Mitford's cremated remains were scattered at sea, as she had requested.

Mizpah Otto had her pet deer Elfina buried at the foot of side-by-side graves in which Mizpah and her husband are now buried. Nearby are the graves of other Otto family members and three Yorkshire terriers. Key West City Cemetery, Key West, Florida.

Composer Gerald Marks wrote his best known song "All of Me" in 1931. Louis Armstrong recorded it, and so did Count Basie and Frank Sinatra, among others. It was the title song of a 1984 Lily Tomlin–Steve Martin movie. When Marks died in 1997 at the age of ninety-six, his final requests were followed: no service was held, his body was cremated, and the epitaph on the urn read "All of Me."

Where to Find the Remains and Burial Sites of Some Famous People

By the mid-nineteenth century cemeteries had become popular attractions. Tourists were encouraged to visit. Guidebooks were written. Maps with the location of the graves of notable people were provided. In 1825 an American visitor to Paris, France, wrote of Père Lachaise, the first modern, garden-style cemetery, "In all respects it very far surpasses anything of the kind I have ever seen." People still visit cemeteries. In 1995 more than eight hundred thousand people visited Père Lachaise. Many travel guidebooks list cemeteries. People also visit other burial sites: the catacombs in Italy and other places, the pyramids in Egypt, the Taj Mahal in India, and the Ming Tombs in China.

People visit burial grounds to seek comfort; to pay homage; to find inspiration; to study inscriptions, art, and architecture; or because they are curious. Tom Weil, who has visited cemeteries for more than twenty-five years, writes in his book *The Cemetery Book*, "How I have enjoyed it all: the quiet country graveyards, the remote and obscure burial grounds, the vast metropolitan necropolises, the gloomy catacombs, and the cheery sun-lit cemeteries, the amusing epitaphs and the ridiculous ones, the

This sign is at the entrance to Rochester Cemetery, Rochester, Iowa, which has been called one of the finest examples of Oak Savannah prairies in the Midwest. Many cemeteries are a wonderful place to see flowers, shrubs, trees, birds, and butterflies.

artful markers and the pompous monuments, and above all, or below all, buried in their subterranean habitats, the people, famous and obscure, celebrated and forgotten, who preceded and predeceased us."

In my experience, many large cemeteries in the United States are generally open seven days a week from 9 A.M. to 5 P.M. Other cemeteries are open all the time. I've located cemeteries by checking a phone book, calling a reference librarian at a library, consulting a guidebook, or just winging it and driving around until I found it. Cemeteries are unique and special places. If you decide to visit the burial sites of some of the famous people who I've listed, don't limit yourself. Once you're there, wander around, explore, and don't be surprised if you discover something else that intrigues you, a likely possibility when you're in a cemetery. Also, don't be surprised if something special happens. Here are two stories about what happened in a cemetery

*On an icy cold day in Febru-
ary, I visited the Princeton
Cemetery in Princeton, New
Jersey, and discovered a tree
that had a large icicle-shaped
purple ornament, some red
bows, and several plastic bags
tied to the branches. One bag
had a photograph, and they all
had messages, including this
one that reads: "September
23/Our 24th Anniversary/My
Darling Bob,/ I miss you
every/ moment of every day!
All my love,/ Forever Yours
Telka*

to an Irish poet, Martin Bakewell, and to my son Stephen and a
group of women who live in a homeless shelter. First the Irish
poet, who I read about in an article by Tom Shea. According to
Shea, Bakewell told him that he found a tour of Dickinson's
house in Amherst, Massachusetts, "haunting in a way that made
me seek out her grave. When I was there a blackbird, a raven,
maybe, sat on her grave and I had this sense of fellowship. I
thought, I have to find out about this woman. . . . As an Irish-

By the 1890s, photographs on gravestones were common in America. Today, most photographs have been baked on enamel or porcelain in the process known as lithophane. The photograph on Gordon Salls's gravestone is of him and his wife, who is still alive. The raccoon, turkey, deer, beaver, and tractor have been colored in a process known as lithochrome. The animals are their natural colors and the tractor is bright blue. Randolph Center Cemetery, Randolph Center, Vermont.

MAN—emphasize that bit—by birth and upbringing I was not educated to take women seriously. But I had this transition when I read her poetry. The more I read the deeper I saw, the more I was moved, the more amazed I was by this poet's insight into people and situations." As for the second story, it starts when a group of women who lived in a homeless shelter decided to visit Madam C. J. Walker's grave in Woodlawn Cemetery in the Bronx, New York. According to Stephen, who worked at the shelter as an adult educator, he and the women had been talking about how Walker, who was born Sarah Breedlove, had started her own line of hair care products, and become one of the richest women in America, probably the first black millionaire-entrepreneur, and an important philanthropist. They also read the book that I wrote, *Madam C. J. Walker: Building a Business*

A portrait of Gary Alan Schauer and a football were etched on his granite gravestone by a memorialist, a person who designs and creates markers for graves. Memorialists use a variety of techniques, including sandblasting, laser etching, and etching by hand using a stylist with a diamond point to produce detailed portraits, scenes, objects, and epitaphs. Pioneer Cemetery, Julian, California.

Empire. Although Woodlawn Cemetery is a long subway ride from the shelter, a group of women eagerly accepted Stephen's offer to go with them to visit Walker's grave. Since I had found the grave only after wandering around a lot myself, the directions I gave Stephen weren't very precise. Nevertheless, Stephen told me, it wasn't long before someone yelled, "Oh, wow, here she is!" After taking pictures of the gravestone, one of the women asked Stephen if he had a copy of my book about Madam Walker. Taking the book out of his backpack, he gave it to her.

Madam C. J. Walker's grave. Woodlawn Cemetery, Bronx, New York.

"We should all sign it and leave it," she said. Then she wrote her message to Madam inside the book—"Thanks for your inspiration"—signed her name, and passed the book to another woman, who wrote, "Thanks for being a strong black woman." After everyone signed the book, the women placed it at the base of the gravestone. Stephen was moved, and so were the women— "Seeing Madam made me feel real peaceful," said one woman. "It was really powerful and inspiring," said another.

Burial Sites of Some Famous People in the United States

Adams, Abigail and John She was a letter writer and wife and mother of U.S. presidents. He was a leader in America's fight for independence and a U.S. president. They are buried in Old Cemetery, Quincy, Massachusetts.

Alcott, Louisa May Writer of fiction for children and adults. Sleepy Hollow Cemetery, Concord, Massachusetts.

Anthony, Susan B. Women's rights advocate. Mount Hope Cemetery, Rochester, New York.

Armstrong, Louis Jazz musician. Flushing Cemetery, Flushing, New York.

Barton, Clara Founder of the Red Cross. North Cemetery, Oxford, Massachusetts.

Bogart, Humphrey Film actor. Forest Lawn Memorial Park, Glendale, California.

Buck, Pearl Nobel Prize winner in literature and a humanitarian. Under an ash tree, Green Hill Farms, Bucks County, Pennsylvania.

Carson, Rachel Marine biologist, ecologist, and science writer. Gate of Heaven Cemetery, Silver Springs, Maryland.

Cather, Willa Novelist, essayist, and short-story writer. Old Town Burial Ground, Jaffrey, New Hampshire.

Chavez, Cesar Labor leader, cofounder of United Farm Workers Union. Rose Garden, United Farm Workers National Headquarters, Kene, California.

Dean, James Film actor. Park Cemetery, Fairmount, Indiana.

Disney, Walt Pioneered animated film cartoon characters. Forest Lawn Memorial Park, Glendale, California.

Dix, Dorothea Social reformer. Mount Auburn Cemetery, Cambridge, Massachusetts.

Flynn, Elizabeth Gurley Political activist, labor leader. Forest Home Cemetery, Forest Park, Illinois.

Zora Neale Hurston's Gravestone, Gate of Heavenly Peace Cemetery, Fort Pierce, Florida.

Two life-size statues of miners stand beside a granite shaft with a bas-relief of Mary Harris "Mother" Jones at her grave. There is also a small granite gravestone on the ground with one word on it— Mother. Jones is buried in Miners Cemetery, Mount Olive, Illinois. It was established in 1898 when other cemeteries refused to bury four workers who were killed by company detectives during a strike at nearby Virden Mines. Jones wanted to be buried there because she wanted "to sleep under the clay with those brave boys."

Franklin, Benjamin Writer, printer, scientist, and statesman. Christ Church Burial Place, Philadelphia, Pennsylvania.

Garland, Judy Singer and film actor. Ferncliff Cemetery, Hartsdale, New York.

Geronimo (Goyahkla) Chief of the Apache Indians. Apache cemetery near Fort Sill, Oklahoma.

Grant, Ulysses Military leader who secured Union victory in the Civil War and a U.S. president. Grant's Tomb, New York City.

Hendrix, Jimi Musician. Greenwood Memorial Park, Renton, Washington.

Holiday, Billie Jazz singer. St. Raymond's Cemetery, Bronx, New York.

Hurston, Zora Neale Folklorist, anthropologist, and novelist. Garden of the Heavenly Rest, Fort Pierce, Florida.

Irving, Washington Author. Old Dutch Church Graveyard, Sleepy Hollow, New York.

Jones, Mary Harris "Mother" Labor organizer. Union Miners' Cemetery, Mount Olive, Illinois.

Keller, Helen Lecturer, author, and advocate for people with disabilities. Cathedral Columbarium, Washington Cathedral, Washington, D.C.

Kennedy, John F., Jacqueline, and Robert U.S. president, first lady, and attorney general and senator of the United States. Arlington National Cemetery, Arlington, Virginia.

King, Martin Luther, Jr. Civil rights leader. South View Cemetery, Atlanta, Georgia.

Lincoln, Abraham U.S. president. Oak Ridge Cemetery, Springfield, Illinois.

Logan, John Native American orator and pacifist. The Logan Memorial, Fort Hill Cemetery, Auburn, New York.

Malcolm X (El Hajj-Malik El Shabazz) Civil rights leader. Ferncliff Cemetery, Hartsdale, New York.

McAuliffe, Christa Teacher. Blossom Hill Cemetery, Concord, New Hampshire.

Mead, Margaret Anthropologist. Buckingham Friends Cemetery, Lahaska, Pennsylvania.

Monroe, Marilyn Film actor. Westwood Memorial Park, Los Angeles, California.

Oakley, Annie Entertainer and sharpshooter. Brock Cemetery, Greenville, Ohio.

O'Keeffe, Georgia Artist. Cremated remains scattered from the top of Cerro Pedernal Mountain in New Mexico.

Perkins, Frances Labor reformer and first woman U.S. cabinet member. River Road Cemetery, Damariscotta, Maine.

Poe, Edgar Allan Short-story writer and poet. Westminster Presbyterian Churchyard, Baltimore, Maryland.

Presley, Elvis Singer. Graceland, Memphis, Tennessee.

Revere, Paul Silversmith and patriot. The Granary, Boston, Massachusetts.

Robinson, Jackie Baseball player. Cypress Hills Cemetery, Queens, New York.

Roosevelt, Franklin Delano and Eleanor He was the longest-serving U.S. president. She was a humanitarian. Franklin D.

John Logan's Memorial, Fort Hill Cemetery, Auburn, New York.

Paul Revere's Gravestone, the Granary, Boston, Massachusetts.

Roosevelt National Historic Site, Hyde Park, New York.

Ruth, Babe Baseball player. Gate of Heaven Cemetery, Hawthorne, New York.

Sacajawea Shoshoni guide for Lewis and Clark. Two places claim her grave: Sacajawea Cemetery, Wind River Reservation, Fort Washakie, Wyoming, and Dakota Memorial Park, Mobridge, South Dakota.

Sitting Bull Chief of the Oglala Sioux Indians. Original grave site is marked at Fort Yates, North Dakota. Supposedly Sitting Bull's body was exhumed and moved to Mobridge, South Dakota.

Stanton, Elizabeth Cady Women's rights advocate and author. Woodlawn Cemetery, Bronx, New York.

Takamine, Jokichi Known as "the father of modern biotechnology" and the person who donated the famous cherry trees to Washington, D.C. Woodlawn Cemetery, Bronx, New York.

Tibbles, Susette La Flesche Known as "Bright Eyes," her Omaha Indian name, she was a reformer and lecturer for Native American rights. Bancroft Cemetery, Bancroft, Nebraska.

Truth, Sojourner Abolitionist and women's rights advocate. Oak Hill Cemetery, Battle Creek, Michigan.

Tubman, Harriet Leader in the Underground Railroad, Civil War scout and spy. Fort Hill Cemetery, Auburn, New York.

Van Lew, Elizabeth Civil War spy. Shockoe Cemetery, Richmond, Virginia.

Behind Harriet Tubman's grave is a tree that was planted when she died, a tradition brought to America by enslaved Africans. Many people believe that if the tree thrives the person's soul is thriving, too. Tubman's tree is spectacular. The last name on her gravestone is from her marriage to Nelson Davis.

Walker, Madam C. J. (Sarah Breedlove) Founder of business empire in hair products, philanthropist. Woodlawn Cemetery, Bronx, New York.

Washington, George Leader of the Continental Army in the Revolutionary War and first U.S. president. Mount Vernon Estate, Mount Vernon, Virginia.

Whitman, Walt Poet. Harleigh Cemetery, Camden, New Jersey.

Epitaphs:
Poignant, Pious, Patriotic,
Historic, and Humorous

If you want to cry, laugh, learn, and be inspired, walk through a cemetery and read the epitaphs, or inscriptions at graves. Epitaphs come in different lengths and with different messages. The ancient Egyptians, Greeks, and Romans carved them on tombs and sarcophagi. The Vikings scratched epitaphs on stones, known as rune stones because they were written in rune, the earliest alphabet used by Teutonic people in Europe. Here are some examples of inscriptions on rune stones in Sweden: "Dan, Huskarl and Sven and Holmfrid, mother and sons, had this stone raised for Ulfrik, their grandfather. . . . Astrid had this stone raised for Osten, her husband. He went to Jerusalem and died in Greece. . . . Karse and Ambjorn had this stone raised in memory of their father, Ulf. God and God's mother have mercy on his soul."

For thousands of years, epitaphs have been written to record facts, express grief, affirm religious beliefs, acknowledge accomplishments and heroic deeds, honor lasting love among families and friends, and sometimes to have the last laugh. Of course, there are exceptions—many Roman epitaphs included a warn-

ing to potential vandals. So did William Shakespeare's epitaph. Because he was a lay rector, Shakespeare had the privilege of being buried in the north side of the chancel of Holy Trinity Church, Stratford-upon-Avon. Perhaps because of the proximity of the charnel-house or the place in which the bones of dead people are piled up—it was reached through a door in the north wall—Shakespeare's epitaph is: "Good friend for Jesus sake forebeare To Digg the Dust Enclosed heare: Bleste be ye Man [tha]t

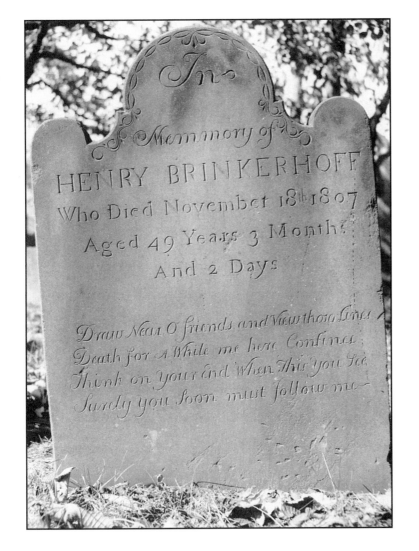

This gravestone has different styles of lettering and a typical epitaph about the inevitability of death. The double m in the word "memmory" is typical of the nonstandard use of spelling, capitalization, and punctuation on old gravestones. The publication of Noah Webster's dictionary in 1823 was the beginning of serious attempts to standardize language usage in America.

spares, and curst be he [tha]t moves my bones." Other epitaphs served as reminders to living people, lest they get too cocky. Here's one from a cemetery in colonial America that is a variation of an ancient epitaph:

> Behold my grave as you pass by.
> As you are living so
> once was I.
> Death suddenly took hold of me,
> And so will be the case with thee.

As I've wandered through cemeteries in the United States I've recorded many epitaphs and organized them into five categories: poignant, pious, patriotic, historic, and humorous. Using those categories as my guide, here is a selection from my collection of American epitaphs:

Poignant

Samuel Clemens, better known as Mark Twain, and his wife, daughters, and sons-in-law are buried in Woodlawn National Cemetery, Elmira, New York, in his wife's family plot. For a daughter who died before him, Clemens wrote this epitaph:

> In the Memory of Jean Lampton Clemens
> A most dear daughter
> Her Desolate Father
> Sets this Stone
> After life's fitful fever
> She sleeps well.

George B. Kupfer died at the age of eight. A lamb carved from stone lies on his gravestone in San Francisco National Cemetery, San Francisco, California:

> *A precious one from us has gone*
> *A voice we loved is still.*
> *A place is vacant in our home*
> *which never can be filled.*

The epitaph for Joseph A. and Phil M. White in St. Peter's Cemetery, Provincetown, Massachusetts, reads:

> *To live in the hearts*
> *we left behind*
> *is not to die.*

On a small, red boulder in Old Deerfield Cemetery, Deerfield, Massachusetts, is carved:

> *Ma Dyed Novem*
> *7 Anno 1696*

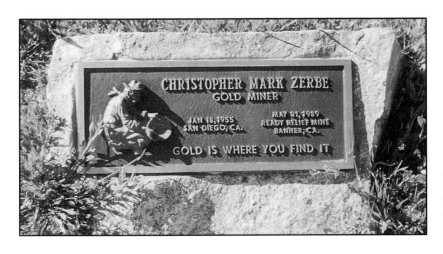

Some epitaphs are philosophical like this one, "Gold is where you find it." Pioneer Cemetery, Julian, California.

In the poignant category I also included epitaphs that deal with the physical realities of death: pain and the causes of death. Here's one from a young woman who is buried in Old Burial Ground, Jaffrey, New Hampshire:

> *Affliction for long time I bore*
> *Physicians were in vain*
> *Till God did please and death did seize*
> *To ease me of my pain.*

This "cause of death" epitaph is found in Mount Pleasant Cemetery, Newark, New Jersey:

A wood marker in Boot Hill Cemetery, Tombstone, Arizona.

> *That Cherry Tree of luscious fruit*
> *Beguiled him too high, a branch did break*
> *and down he fell and broke his neck and*
> *died July 13th, 1862.*

Here are excerpts from more "cause of death" epitaphs: "killed by fall from a horse . . . ," "killed by a falling tree . . . ," "falling from a stagecoach . . . ," "died of the prevailing fever . . . ," "drowned in the Savannah River . . . ," "legally hanged . . . ," and "receiv'd a mortal wound on his head by the falling of a weight from the Bell as he was about to enter the Church to attend a divine worship."

Some poignant epitaphs are very sweet and romantic. Here's one in Brookside Cemetery, Englewood, New Jersey:

> *When I Held You Tight*
> *All The Stars Seemed So Much Brighter*
> *They Lit Up The Night*

Pious

Many epitaphs reflect religious beliefs and practices. People express their faith in a variety of ways. Typically these epitaphs are straightforward, like this one:

> *Pray for me, As I will for thee*
> *That we may meet in heaven.*

An epitaph from a grave in Boca Raton Memorial Cemetery and Mausoleum, Boca Raton, Florida, reads:

Murphy Family Gravestone, Brookside Cemetery, Englewood, New Jersey.

In God we trust
To God we pray
With God we live

Bible verses are frequently used. Here are three that are inscribed on a headstone for a family in Woodside Cemetery, Dumont, New Jersey:

Blessed are the dead which die in the Lord. Rev. 14:13
We which have believed do enter into rest. Heb. 4:3
Waiting for the coming of our Lord Jesus Christ. 1 Cor. 1:7

Patriotic

Until the late nineteenth century, patriotic themes were not generally expressed in epitaphs. The drama and trauma of the Civil

War changed that. Patriotic epitaphs began to appear that honored, and perhaps justified a soldier's "sacrifice for his country." In the years after the Civil War, patriotism proliferated in cemeteries throughout the United States: countless numbers of statues of soldiers were erected, stately monuments were constructed, patriotic symbols—eagles, flags, and weapons—appeared, and patriotic epitaphs were placed at graves.

According to his headstone, Frank Van Wetering was twenty-four years old when he died, a soldier in World War I. His epitaph in Catholic Cemetery in Hackensack, New Jersey, reads:

Military monuments are a common sight in cemeteries. This statue of a Civil War soldier is in Spring Grove Cemetery, Wisconsin Dells, Wisconsin.

> *In Loving Memory of Pvt. Frank J. Van Wetering, Company C, Sixth Engineers, United States Army. Born February 8, 1894. Fought in the Battle of Picardy and the Marne. Killed in Action at the Battle of the Marne, France, July 15, 1918. He Bravely Laid Down His Life for the Cause of His Country. His Name Will Ever Remain Fresh in the Hearts of His Friends and Comrades. The Record of His Honorable Service Will Be Preserved in the Archives of the American Expeditionary Forces.*

Elizabeth Van Lew was a Union spy during the Civil War. After her death admirers placed a grayish beige and rose-colored boulder on her grave in Shockoe Cemetery, Richmond, Virginia. A bronze plaque was attached to the boulder with the epitaph:

> *She risked everything that is dear to man—friends, fortune, comfort, health, life itself—all for the one absorbing desire of her heart, that slavery might be abolished and the Union preserved.*

Historic

All sorts of people have had history-making events noted in their epitaphs. Some of the names and events are in the history books; others aren't. But they all reflect people's determination and drive to make a difference in the world.

In Forest Home Cemetery, Forest Park, Illinois, there's a page from labor history. Elizabeth Gurley Flynn is buried there with the epitaph:

The Rebel Girl Fighter for Working Class Emancipation

A piece of African-American history is revealed in the epitaph for Amos Fortune (1710–1801), Old Burial Ground, Jaffrey, New Hampshire:

> *Amos Fortune, who was born free in Africa,*
> *a slave in America, he purchased liberty,*
> *professed Christianity, lived reputably,*
> *and died hopefully.*

It is also found in Harriet Tubman's epitaph, which is on the back of her headstone in Fort Hill Cemetery, Auburn, New York:

> *Heroine of the Underground Railroad*
> *Nurse and Scout in the Civil War*
> *Born about 1820 in Maryland*
> *Died March 10, 1913, at Auburn, New York*
> *"Servant of God, Well Done"*

Music history is found on W. C. Handy's gravestone in Woodlawn Cemetery in the Bronx, New York. Known as "the Father of the Blues," Handy's epitaph isn't in letters, it's in musical notes—the opening notes of his classic composition "Saint Louis Blues." Superimposed over the music is an engraving of a trumpet.

The struggle for women's rights and equality is noted in Elizabeth Cady Stanton's epitaph in Woodlawn Cemetery, Bronx, New York:

> *. . . Called Woman's Rights Convention*
> *First in History at Seneca Falls, New York, July 19, 1848*
> *Demanded Votes for Women. . . .*

In the same cemetery a monument marks the graves of Carrie Chapman Catt, who spearheaded the final drive for woman's suffrage, and her lieutenant Mary Garrett Hay. They have a joint epitaph that reads:

In 1881, fifteen-year-old Kate Shelley's heroic act prevented a railroad tragedy. Shelley died in 1912 and forty-four years later the Order of Railway Conductors and Brakemen erected this memorial with a brief history of her deed at her grave. Sacred Heart Cemetery, Boone, Iowa.

Here lie two united together in friendship
For thirty-eight years through constant service to a great cause.

The dedication of a scientist is also noted in Woodlawn Cemetery in the epitaph for Hideyo Noguchi, a bacteriologist who discovered the causes of several diseases, including syphilis.

Through devotion to science
he lived and died for humanity.

The history of the United States as a nation of immigration, emigration, and diversity is also reflected in epitaphs. I've seen epitaphs written in many languages, including Swedish, Greek, Hebrew, Yiddish, Spanish, Russian, Chinese, Japanese, Serbo-Croatian, Arabic, and Italian. I've seen birthplaces inscribed on headstones, including Crete on a headstone in New Jersey; Springfield, Illinois, on a headstone in Nebraska; and Bosnia-Herzegovina on a headstone in California. The struggles of pioneers is reflected in epitaphs on graves along the

An epitaph in Spanish. In English it reads: "Mami, when you left, you took half my life." Pioneer Cemetery, Watsonville, California.

"Rachel taken sick in the morning, died in the night," is how Nathan Pattison recorded the death of his wife, Rachel Warren Pattison. Nathan and Rachel were married on April 3, 1849, in Randolph County, Illinois. A week later, they set out with Nathan's parents, William and Mary, five brothers, and other relatives to take the trail to Oregon. They reached Ash Hollow in Nebraska on June 18, the day after three of their oxen ate poisonous weeds and died. On June 19, Rachel died of cholera. According to Nathan's father's diary, "Rachel was taken with Colara [cholera] and died by 11 at night . . . [we buried her] on the left side of the hollow as you go round the bluff up the River on the second bank placing a gravestone at her head." Today Rachel's gravestone is on display in a large stone monument in Ash Hollow Cemetery that was laid out by Dennis and W. H. Gilliard in the late 1880s around her grave. The inscription on Rachel's gravestone is: "1849 / Rachel E. Pattison / aged 18 / June 19th 49."

routes that they traveled on foot, on horseback, and in covered wagons.

Humorous

I had read that there were gravestones with the epitaph "I told you I was sick." However, I did not really believe they existed until I found this one in Princeton Cemetery, Princeton, New Jersey. Subsequently, I found the same epitaph on B. P. "Pearl" Roberts's gravestone in Key West City Cemetery, Key West, Florida.

Here are some epitaphs that made me smile, even laugh.

An epitaph on a gravestone in Enfield, Connecticut:

> *In memory of*
> *Deacon Ezekiel Pease*
> *who died June 20th, A.D. 1799*
> *Aged 89 years wanting 12 days.*
> *What lies here is only the pod;*
> *He shelled out his Pease and went to his God.*

Orlando "Junie" Minetto set up lobster tanks and sold live lobsters to restaurants. After he died, his grown children had an epitaph about his favorite restaurant inscribed on his gravestone: "I'd rather be at the Lounge." Mount Caramel Cemetery, Tenafly, New Jersey.

According to his epitaph, Charles A. Stubbs, who is buried in Boca Raton Municipal Cemetery, Boca Raton, Florida, has "Gone Fishing." As for Dutch Conkling, who is buried in Brookside Cemetery, Englewood, New Jersey, he has "Gone Bowling Again."

The source of this epitaph is unknown, but it reads:

> Soon ripe
>
> Soon rotten
>
> Soon gone
>
> But not forgotten.

A woman in New Jersey had a recipe carved in her gravestone along with the words:

> *I always said*
> *the only way you would*
> *get this recipe*
> *was over my dead body.*

This epitaph is in the cemetery in Skaneateles, New York:

> *Underneath this pile of stones*
> *Lies all that's left of Sally Jones.*
> *Her name was Lord, it was not Jones,*
> *But Jones was used to rhyme with stones.*

Common Carvings on Gravestones

Symbol	Meaning
Anchor	Grave of a seafarer and/or a symbol of hope
Angel	Afterlife in heaven
Bamboo	Longevity
Broken column	Mourning
Butterfly	Resurrection
Clasped hands	Farewell and friendship
Crosses	Symbol of Christianity
Celtic	Immortality
Greek or Latin	Christianity
Maltese	Bravery
Crown	Reward in heaven or a noble person
Dove	Holy Spirit or peace
Dragon	Eternity or royalty
Effigy	Remembering the dead person with an image
Flowers	Love, beauty, brevity of life

Heart	Love
Hourglass	Inevitability of death
Ivy	Remembrance or friendship
Lamb	Purity, innocence; typically used for a child
Lamp	Knowledge of God
Lily	Purity
Lion or Foo dog	For Chinese people one of the four animals of power, energy, and bravery
Nature images, including leaves and trees	Love of nature
Peony	Honor, love, or affection
Pheasant	Beauty and good fortune
Praying hands	Piety
Scythe	Life cut short
Sheaves of wheat	Abundant life or final harvest
Skull with or without crossbones	Finality of death
Star of David	Symbol of Judaism
Tree trunks with broken branches	Life cut short by death
Urn	Death and mourning
Violets	Humility
Willow	Weeping and sorrow of survivors

Chronology

B.C.E.

70,000
Burial sites of Paleolithic people from this time period have been excavated by archaeologists.

7000
In Jericho dead people were buried under the floor without their skulls, which were restored as part of a burial ritual.

6000
People lived in settlements and cities, including Catal Hüyük in Anatolia in Turkey and Khirokitia in Cyprus, where cemeteries have been excavated.

In Egypt dead bodies were buried in the sand of the desert, where they would be preserved for thousands of years.

about 2600
Earliest known attempts to artificially create mummies in Egypt.

about 1000
Adena and Hopewell people began building burial mounds in what is now the Ohio Valley.

1000
Greeks began cremating their dead.

about 600
Romans adopted cremation. (Later, Romans in the Republic were buried, but the Emperor Augustus changed the system back to cremation because he feared the effects on health from the overcrowded common burial pits.)

352
An elaborate tomb was built for King Mausolus at Halicarnassus in Caria. Called one of the Seven Wonders of the World, the word *mausoleum* is derived from his tomb.

332–30
Mummification became universal in Egypt.

mid-200s
Sarcophagi, or stone tombs, were first constructed.

early 200s
Coffins were first used in Sumer and Egypt.

44
To determine the cause of Julius Caesar's death, the Roman physician Antistius performed one of the earliest recorded forensic examinations. He concluded that only one of the twenty-three stab wounds on Caesar's body was fatal—the one to his chest.

C.E.

200
Early Christians began using catacombs on the outskirts of Rome.

400
Catacombs all but forgotten.

1247
Hsi Yüan Ch'i Lü (The Washing Away of Unjust Wrongs), a Chinese handbook on autopsies, was published.

1318
Ossuary at Kutná Hora in the Czech Republic was built.

1578
Catacombs rediscovered in Rome.

1630
Empress Mumtaz Mahal died after requesting that her husband not remarry and that he build her the most magnificent tomb the world had seen. Some twenty years later the Taj Mahal was completed.

1631
Ancient Funerall Monuments published by John Weever, first work in English on epitaphs.

1698
The term undertaker was now in use.

1768
The earliest record of an undertaker in the Thirteen Colonies: Blanch White, who set up a New York City business that combined upholstering and undertaking. Her advertisement: "All kinds of Field Equipage, Drums, Etc. Funerals furnishe'd with all things necessary and proper Attendance as in England."

1804

Père Lachaise, the first "garden" or "rural" cemetery, opened in Paris.

1831

Mount Auburn Cemetery opened in Cambridge, Massachusetts, and the "garden" or "rural" cemetery movement began in the United States.

1863

First large military cemetery was established in the United States.

1869

First serious experiments in modern cremation technique were carried out in Italy.

1878

The Undertaker, the first textbook devoted to embalming in the United States, was published.

1885

The term *funeral director* coined in the United States.

1917

In California, Hubert Eaton began to create Forest Lawn as a memorial park.

1968

The 22nd World Medical Assembly published standards for diagnosing death by brain criteria.

1981

In the United States guidelines for determining death were proposed in the Uniform Determination of Death Act, which has become law in many states.

1993

Many graves in a cemetery in Hardin, Missouri, were washed away when the Missouri River flooded in the summer. It cost $500,000 to retrieve and identify corpses. However, 127 corpses were never recovered, and 470 remain unidentified.

1996

The mummified body of a five-thousand-year-old Inca girl was discovered entombed in the ice on Mount Ampato, near Arequipa, Peru.

1997

A rocket with the cremated remains of twenty-four people was launched into outer space.

Glossary

Autopsy: An inside and outside examination of a dead body to determine the cause of death and/or to study the effects of a disease or injury. An autopsy is also called a postmortem examination, known as a "post."

Barrow: A large mound of earth or stones piled on top of dead bodies.

Bier: The stand on which a corpse, coffin, or casket is placed.

Body: Another word for a corpse.

Brain-dead: Traditionally the term meant the determination of death when no activity could be detected in a person's brain. Currently the term *brain death* has been replaced by the more precise term *death by brain criteria*.

Casket: A rectangular-shaped burial container for the human body. It is typically fancier than a coffin.

Catacomb: An underground network of corridors and rooms that were once used as burial places. Graves were cut into the walls.

Cemetery: Burial site in the earth. Early Christian writers coined the word *cemetery* as a euphemism to refer to where dead people were buried. It comes from the Greek word *koimeterion*, meaning "to sleep." The first recorded use of the word in English was 1387. The word *graveyard* came into use in the early nineteenth century.

Cerecloth: A cloth used to cover a corpse. It was treated with a wax or gummy material in order to hold the cloth close to the body.

Charon: An old boatman in Greek mythology who ferried the souls of dead people across the river Styx or the Acheron River to Hades.

Coffin: A traditional wedge-shaped burial receptacle for the human body.

Columbarium: A structure containing recessed niches for urns that contain cremains, or cremated remains.

Corpse: Originally used to signify the body of a living person, *corpse* is now used to mean a dead body.

Cremated remains: The bone fragments remaining after cremation.

Cremation: The process of using heat to reduce a corpse to bone fragments.

Crematorium: The place that contains the furnace in which bodies are cremated. Also called a crematory.

Cryonics: The practice of freezing at extremely low temperatures the bodies of people who have died of a disease with the hope that the body might be revived and healed if a cure is discovered.

Crypt: A vault with an arched or domed ceiling or a chamber in which a body is placed. A crypt is usually totally or partly underground. Historically crypts were often built beneath the main floor of a church, usually as a burial place. Today the drawers that hold bodies in aboveground mausoleums are often called crypts.

Decomposition: The natural process through which bodies break down to organic and inorganic parts and eventually disappear.

Dissect: To cut apart a cadaver in order to examine and analyze its parts.

Elegy: A poem or song to honor a dead person.

Embalming: A process to preserve a body.

Epitaph: An inscription or a message on a tomb or gravestone.

Eulogy: A speech that honors a person.

Exhumation: Removing a corpse from a grave.

Floater: Bodies submersed in water for a long enough period of time to have developed enough gas in the abdomen to float to the surface.

Funeral: A ceremony held for a dead person. The body is present.

Grave: An excavation for burial of a body.

Inhumation: Burial in the ground.

Mausoleum: A large tomb built aboveground.

Memorial park: Cemetery where graves are marked with markers flush to the ground.

Memorial service: A ceremonial held for a dead person. The body is not present.

Morgue: A place where corpses are kept until they are claimed or released for burial.

Mummy: A corpse whose skin has been preserved over a skeleton, either through natural or artificial processes.

Necropolis: A Greek word meaning "city of the dead," which is what scholars typically call cemeteries in ancient cities.

Ossuary: Depository for the bones of dead people.

Pyre: An open fire used to cremate bodies.

Rigor mortis: Stiffening of the body after death.

Sarcophagus: A stone coffin. Ancient people excavated stone and carved coffins for dead people. Because materials in the stone were believed to eat the corpse, the coffin was called a sarcophagus, from the Greek word *sarkos*, meaning "flesh," and *phagos*, meaning "I eat."

Shroud: A white garment in which corpses are buried.

Thanatology: The study of death.

Tomb: A structure or excavation in which a corpse is buried. It can be entirely aboveground or wholly or partly in the ground.

Tumulus: A hill that was built over a grave.

Urn: A receptacle designed to permanently encase cremated remains.

Viewing: A burial ritual during which friends see the corpse and visit with the family.

Wake: The time when people watch over a dead body before it is buried.

Bibliography

There are many resources about death. The materials in this bibliography are just the beginning of a list that could go on and on! Clearly death is a subject that has captured the interest and imagination of many people.

Books

Aries, Phillipe. *Western Attitudes Toward Death: From the Middle Ages to the Present*. Baltimore: The Johns Hopkins University Press, 1974.

————. *The Hour of Our Death*. Translated by Helen Weaver. New York: Alfred A. Knopf, 1981.

————, and Georges Duby, eds. *A History of Private Lives*. Cambridge: The Belknap Press of Harvard University, 1987.

Ball, James Moores. *The Body Snatchers: Doctors, Grave Robbers and the Law*. New York: Dorset Press, 1989.

Ballantine, Betty and Ian. *The Native Americans*. Atlanta: Turner Publishing, 1993.

Barber, P. *Vampires, Burial and Death: Folklore and Reality:* New Haven: Yale University Press, 1988.

Bendann, E. *Death Customs: An Analytical Study of Burial Rites*. New York: Alfred A. Knopf, 1930.

Bergman, Edward F. *Woodlawn Remembers*. Utica, N.Y.: North Country Books, 1988.

Bertman, Sandra L. *Facing Death: Images, Insights, and Interventions*. New York: Hemisphere, 1991.

Burns, Stanley B. *Sleeping Beauty: A History of Memorial Photography in America*. Altadena, Calif.: Twelvetrees Press, 1990.

Coffin, Margaret M. *Death in Early America*. New York: Elsevier/Nelson Books, 1976.

Curl, J. S. *The Victorian Celebration of Death*. Detroit: Partridge Press, 1972.

DuBois, P. M. *The Hospice Way of Death*. New York: Human Sciences Press, 1980.

Ellis, Nancy, and Parker Hayden. *Here Lies America: A Collection of Notable Graves*. New York: Hawthorn Books, 1978.

Elsen, Albert E. *Purposes of Art*. New York: Holt, Rinehart and Winston, 1967.

Enright, D. J. *The Oxford Book of Death*. Oxford: Oxford University Press, 1983.

Forbes, Harriette Merrifield. *Gravestones of Early New England and the Men Who Made Them, 1653–1800*. Rev. ed. Brooklyn: Center for Thanatology Research and Education, 1989.

Garlake, Peter. *The Kingdoms of Africa*. New York: Peter Bedrick Books, 1990.

Garland, Robert. *The Greek Way of Death*. Ithaca, N.Y.: Cornell University Press, 1985.

Genovese, Eugene D. *Roll, Jordan, Roll: The World the Slaves Made*. New York: Vintage Books, 1974.

Habenstein, Robert W., and William M. Lamers. *The History of American Funeral Directing*. Milwaukee: Bulfin, 1962.

———. *Funeral Customs the World Over*. 4th ed. Milwaukee: Bulfin, 1994.

Halporn, Roberta. *Gods, Ghosts and Ancestors*. Brooklyn: Center for Thanatology Research, 1984.

———. *Lessons from the Dead*. Brooklyn: Highly Specialized Promotions, 1979.

Herzog, Edgar. *Psyche and Death*. New York: G. P. Putnam's Sons, 1967.

Huntington, Richard, and Peter Metcalf. *Celebrations of Death: The Anthropology of Mortuary Rituals*. Cambridge: Cambridge University Press, 1979.

Iserson, Kenneth. *Death to Dust: What Happens to Dead Bodies?* Tucson, Ariz.: Galen Press, 1994.

Jackson, Charles O., ed. *Passing: The Vision of Death in America*. Westport, Conn.: Greenwood Press, 1977.

Jackson, Kenneth T., and Camilo José Vergara. *Silent Cities: The Evolution of the American Cemetery*. New York: Princeton Architectural Press, 1989.

Jones, Barbara. *Design for Death*. Indianapolis: Bobbs-Merrill, 1967.

Kalish, Richard A. *Death and Dying: Views from Many Cultures*. Farmingdale, N.Y.: Baywood Publishing Co., 1977.

Kastenbaum, Robert J. *Death, Society & Human Experience*. Saint Louis: C. V. Mosby, 1977.

Kübler-Ross, Elisabeth. *Death: The Final Stage of Growth*. Englewood Cliffs, N.J.: Prentice-Hall, 1975.

———. *On Death and Dying*. New York: Macmillan, 1969.

Kumar, Radha. *The History of Doing*. New Dehli: Kali for Women, 1993.

Lai, T. C. *To the Yellow Springs: The Chinese View of Death*. Hong Kong: Joint Publishing Co. and Kelly & Walsh, 1983.

Lamm, Maurice. *The Jewish Way in Death and Mourning*. New York: Jonathan David Publishers, 1969.

Lovell, John, Jr. *Black Song: The Forge and the Flame*. New York: Macmillan, 1972.

Miller, Randall M., and John David Smith. *Dictionary of Afro-American Slavery*. New York: Greenwood Press, 1988.

Mitford, Jessica. *The American Way of Death*. New York: Simon & Schuster, 1963.

Morley, John. *Death, Heaven and the Victorians*. Pittsburgh: University of Pittsburgh Press, 1971.

Murphy, Dervla. *Muddling Through Madagascar*. New York: Overlook Press, 1989.

Nagy, Maria H. *The Meaning of Death*. New York: McGraw-Hill, 1965.

Nuland, Sherwin B. *How We Die*. New York: Alfred A. Knopf, 1993.

Oxenstierna, Eric. *The Norsemen*. Greenwich, Conn.: New York Graphic Society Publishers, 1965.

Paludan, Ann. *The Imperial Ming Tombs*. New Haven: Yale University Press, 1981.

Parrinder, Geoffrey. *African Mythology*. New York: Peter Bedrick Books, 1987.

Puckle, Bertram. *Funeral Customs*. London: T. Werner Laurie, 1926.

Putnam, James. *Mummy*. New York: Alfred A. Knopf, 1993.

Quigley, Christine. *The Corpse: A History*. Jefferson, N.C.: McFarland Company, 1996.

———. *Death Dictionary*. Jefferson, N.C.: McFarland Company, 1994.

Rakoff, Vivian. *Death in American Experience*. New York: Schocken Books, 1974.

Riemer, Jack, ed. *Jewish Reflections on Death*. New York: Schocken Books, 1974.

Ronan, Margaret, and Eve Ronan. *Death Around the World*. New York: Scholastic Book Services, 1978.

Sarapin, Janice Kohl. *Old Burial Grounds of New Jersey*. New Brunswick, N.J.: Rutgers University Press, 1994.

Selzer, Richard. *Mortal Lessons: Notes of the Art of Surgery*. New York: Simon & Schuster, 1987.

Shneidman, Edwin S. *Death: Current Perspectives*. Palo Alto, Calif.: Mayfield Publishing Co., 1976.

Southern, Eileen. *The Music of Black Americans: A History*. 3rd edition. New York: W. W. Norton, 1997.

Stannard, David E., ed. *Death in America*. Philadelphia: University of Pennsylvania Press, 1975.

Toynbee, J. M. C. *Death and Burial in the Roman World*. Ithaca, N.Y.: Cornell University Press, 1971.

Thompson, Robert Farris. *Flash of the Spirit: African & Afro-American Art & Philosophy*. New York: Random House, 1983.

Vigarello, Georges. *Concepts of Cleanliness*. Cambridge: Cambridge University Press, 1988.

Walker, G. A. *Gatherings from Graveyards*. New York: Arno Press, 1977.

Waugh, Evelyn. *The Loved One*. London: Chapman & Hall, 1948.

Weil, Thomas. *The Cemetery Book: Graveyards, Catacombs, and Other Travel Haunts Around the World*. New York: Hippocrene Books, 1992.

Articles

Colker, David. "Rest in Space." *Los Angeles Times* (July 25, 1996): 2.

Colman, Penny. "Staring Death in the Face." *Woman's Day* (May 1990): 132.

"Cremains of the Day." *Sports Illustrated* (April 1996): 10.

Daunt, Tina. "Farewell to the Forgotten." *Los Angeles Times* (Nov. 27, 1993): 1

Dolan, Carrie. "Burying Tradition, More People Opt for 'Fun' Funerals." *Wall Street Journal* (May 20, 1993): A1.

French, Howard W. "A Whimsical Coffin?" *The New York Times* (Dec. 18, 1995): 4.

Gibson, David. "Bishops May Ask Vatican to Permit Ashes at Mass." *The Record* (Sept. 6, 1996): 13.

Goldberg, Carey. "Now on Sale: Lenin-Style Embalming." *Los Angeles Times* (Jan. 22, 1994): A6.

Grady, Denise. "Research Uses Grow for Virtual Cadavers." *The New York Times* (Oct. 8, 1996): C1, C7.

Grant, Steve. "Rediscovering Cedar Hill." *The Hartford Courant* (June 18, 1996): 1, A8.

Greenwald, Marilyn. "Robert Pugh." *Stone in America* (Sept. 1988): 41–47.

Gutierrez, Lisa. "Garden Plots." *Democrat and Chronicle* (July 20, 1996): P1, C6.

Haass, Jane Glenn. "Memorable Memories." *The Des Moines Register* (May 20, 1997): 3T.

Hanken, James. "The Art of the Skull." *Natural History* (Oct. 1996): 34–39.

Hart, Anne. "Tyrone Ponders Future of Cemetery." *Atlanta Constitution* (Feb. 15, 1996): 10.

Hellman, Peter. "Where History Is at Rest." *The New York Times* (Sept. 6, 1996): C1, C20.

Hinman, Johanna. "If You Have a Lemon, Make Lemonade; If You Have Bones . . ." *The Prague Post* (July 10–16, 1996): 6a.

Jordan, Mary, and Kevin Sullivan. "Saving Face: Japanese Can Rent Mourners, Relatives, Friends, Even Enemies to Buff an Image." *The Washington Post* (Sept. 8, 1995): A1.

Lambert, Bruce. "Recalling the Meaning Behind Memorial Day." *The New York Times* (May 24, 1996): 35.

Marriott, Michel. "Touched by Death, Hip-Hop Turns to Dirges." *The New York Times* (Oct. 13, 1996): 11.

Mitford, Jessica. "Death, Incorporated." *Vanity Fair* (March 1997): 110, 115–116, 118, 120, 131.

Morrison, Jim. "A Resting Place in Space." *The New York Times* (Sept. 17, 1995): 51.

Mufson, Steven. "China Robbed of Its Rich Past." *The Washington Post* (Sept. 13, 1995): 13.

Palazzolo, Rosa. "Graveyards Are Classes for the Study of Death." *Brooklyn Paper Publication* (Nov. 2, 1995): 3.

Rivenburg, Roy. "The Iceman Goeth." *Los Angeles Times* (Mar. 2, 1994): E1.

———. "Return of the Mummy." *Los Angeles Times* (Jan. 27, 1993): E1.

Robinson, Charles T. "The Words on Nelly's Tombstone." *Yankee* (Jan. 1994): 18.

Rozbruch, Roslyn. "A Chance to Say Goodbye: Children Shouldn't Automatically Be Excluded from Funerals and Wakes." *Los Angeles Times* (June 2, 1996): E3.

Shea, Tom. "Emily Casts a Long Shadow for Irish Author." *Springfield Union* (Sept. 10, 1996): 3.

Sherman, Mark. "The Neighbors Will Burn with Envy." *Business Week* (Sept. 26, 1994): 8.

Stout, David. "Reflections for Halloween: Messages from the Grave, If Not Beyond It." *The New York Times* (Oct. 30, 1994): 7.

Tannenbaum, Jeffrey A. "High Costs of Dying Give This Franchiser an Opening." *Wall Street Journal* (April 26, 1993): 2.

Toolen, Tom. "History in Repose." *The Record* (Oct. 28, 1995): SL1, SL4.

Vial, Debra Lynn. "Putting Some Life into Funerals." *The Record* (July 8, 1996): 1, 5.

Weiss, Ray. "History in Stone." *Rockland Journal-News* (Sept. 29, 1996): C1, C12.

Wilford, John Noble. "Cave Filled with Glowing Skulls: A Pre-Columbian Palace of the Dead." *The New York Times* (Oct. 4, 1994): 5.

———. "Mummy Tells Story of a Sacrifice, Scientists Say." *The New York Times* (May 22, 1996): 13.

Winokur, Julie, and Ed Kashi. "City of the Dead." *Aubudon* (July 1994): 70.

Videos

New England Gravestones and the Stories They Tell. Greenfield, Mass.: The Association for Gravestone Studies, 1990.

Web Sites

The Cemetery Gate: http://alpha.vaxxine.com/info/memorial.html
The Virtual Memorial Garden: http://www.catless.ncl.ac.uk/VMG
World Gardens Virtual Cemetery: http://www.worldgardens.com
Worldwide Cemetery: http://www.cemetery.org

Other Resources

Educators' Kit. Des Plaines, Ill.: Monument Builders of North America, 1995.

Notes

All of the books and articles that are cited in the text are listed in the bibliography. All the names of people in the text are real, with the exception of "Janet" and "Bill" in Ann Sparanese's account of her trip to the morgue. In doing my research I found the following books particularly helpful: *Death to Dust: What Happens to Dead Bodies?* by Kenneth Iserson, *Death and Dying: Views from Many Cultures* by Richard A. Kalish, *Celebrations of Death: The Anthropology of Mortuary Rituals* by Richard Huntington and Peter Metcalf, *Death in Early America* by Margaret M. Coffin, *Death in America* by David Stannard, and *Funeral Customs the World Over* by Robert W. Habenstein and William M. Lamers.

Information about Dr. Perry in Chapter 1 came from two sources: *Old Churchyard: St. Helena's Episcopal Church, Beaufort, South Carolina*, edited by James Cawood Presgraves and S. Louise Presgraves and *Tales of Beaufort* by Nell S. Graydon, which were sent to me by Gail and Robert Taylor from Beaufort, South Carolina. Also in Chapter 1, the quote from the Buddha is from *What Buddhists Believe* by K. Sri Dhammannanda. The information about the Viele Memorial is from *Home at Rest: The Story of the West Point Cemetery* by Thomas E. O'Neil. Information about Maria Nagy's research, which appears in Chapter 2, is available in several sources, including *Death, Society & Human Experience* by Robert Kastenbaum. Descriptions of the waiting mortuaries in Chapter 2 are from Barbara Jones's book *Design for Death*. The material about the Parsi in Chapter 4 is from Kenneth Iserson's book *Death to Dust*. Joseph Carr's quotes in Chapters 4 and 5 are from Jessica Mitford's book *The American Way of Death*. *Death in Early America* by Margaret Coffin was my source for the story about the Hillers, David Evans's diary entries, and L. M. Sargent's account in Chapter 5. Material about the Vikings came primarily from Eric Oxenstierna's book *The Norsemen*. Tom Weil's book, *The Cemetery Book*, provided some of the information for the section "When I Die." Information in "When I Die" and Chapter 1 about the graves in the Key West City Cemetery are from "Historic Key West City Cemetery: A Self-Guided Tour," a pamphlet published by the Historic Florida Keys Foundation.

Photo Credits

Cover:

Penny Colman

Title Page and Dedication:

Penny Colman

Preface:

4: Linda Hickson; *5, 6, 7, 8, 10, 11,13*: Penny Colman

Chapter 1:

16: author's collection; *17*: National Library of Medicine; *19, 21*: Penny Colman; *24, 25*: National Library of Medicine; *26*: Penny Colman

Chapter 2:

30: Penny Colman; *32*: Ohio Historical Society; *34, 36*: Library of Congress; *37, 38, 39, 40*: Penny Colman; *41*: Brooklyn Museum of Art; *42*: Penny Colman

Chapter 3:

45: National Library of Medicine; *47*: Katrin de Haën; *48*: Penny

Colman; *50*: National Library of Medicine; *53, 58*: Library of Congress

Chapter 4:

62: author's collection; *63*: Penny Colman; *65*: Library of Congress; *68*: National Library of Medicine; *69*: Library of Congress; *72*: Penny Colman

Chapter 5:

75, 76: Penny Colman; *78, 79*: Library of Congress; *82*: Penny Colman; *83*: Library of Congress; *84*: Penny Colman; *85*: Lindsay Koehler; *86, 88*: Penny Colman; *89*: United States Naval Academy

Chapter 6:

92, 93: Penny Colman; *94*: Collection of Marlise Johnson; *95*: John Granberry; *96*: Library of Congress; *101*: Penny Colman; *102*: Barbara Kiefer; *104, 105*: Jonathan Colman and Katrin de Haën; *106*: collection of Frances Treanor; *107, 109, 110, 112, 113, 114, 115, 116*: Penny Colman; *117*: photo by Penny Colman from the collection of Brookside Cemetery, Englewood, New Jersey

Chapter 7:

120: Library of Congress; *121*: Brooklyn Museum of Art, Gift of Lester Wunderman; *123*: Library of Congress; *125*: author's collection; *126, 128, 130, 132, 133*: Library of Congress; *135*: author's collection; *136*: Penny Colman; *137*: photo by Penny Colman from the collection of the Center of Thanatology Research and Education; *139*: Penny Colman

Chapter 8:

142, 143, 144: Penny Colman; *145*: National Library of Medicine; *146*: photo by Penny Colman from the collection of Gay Culverhouse; *147, 148*: Library of Congress; *150*: Penny Colman; *151*: Carol A. Perkins

When I Die:

155: Clyde A. Chamberlin; *159*: Penny Colman

Where to Find the Remains:

162, 163, 164, 165, 166, 167: Penny Colman; *168*: Illinois Labor History Society; *169* (upper): Penny Colman; *169* (lower): Katrin de Haën; *170*: Penny Colman

Epitaphs:

173, 175: Penny Colman; *176*: Library of Congress; *178, 179, 181, 182, 183, 184, 185*: Penny Colman

Common Carvings:

188: Penny Colman

Index